"Reading is the necessary backdrop to relevant twenty-first-century preaching. There is no shortcut or substitute. When the gospel and the preacher's personal faith and experience are informed by wide, disciplined, varied, and sustained reading, lively and compelling sermons will be the result. Cornelius Plantinga, an avid and creative reader himself, provides the community of preachers with a very valuable resource and the impetus for all of us to *read, read, read.*"

— JOHN BUCHANAN
editor/publisher of
The Christian Century

"Why don't preachers read more? Preachers are writers who produce more content each week than the average newspaper columnist. Why don't we ravenously read in order to feed the beast of each Sunday's deadline? The truth is that a million pressing callings invade the small space that pastors reserve for reading. And so I give thanks for the deep reading that Cornelius Plantinga has done over the years, and for this gentle guide to words that are worth reading."

— LILLIAN DANIEL
author of *When "Spiritual but
Not Religious" Is Not Enough*

"This treasure of a book by Neal Plantinga offers substantial help to a generation of young preachers (and older ones too) who have not fully grasped the importance of furnishing the mind with great literary writing. . . . Plantinga is discerning, witty, humane, up-to-date, and profoundly pastoral. I urgently recommend this ear-opening book to a host of readers — including not only preachers but also those who listen to preaching, for they will be enlarged by it as well."

— FLEMING RUTLEDGE
author of *And God Spoke to
Abraham: Preaching from the
Old Testament*

"This beautifully written gem of a book admirably fulfills its sign function by pointing not at itself but at the thing it is about — other people's books. Plantinga makes as good a case as I have come across for the importance of reading *many* books to enrich the preaching of the Christian's *one* book. Here is no recipe for pretty preaching, which only distracts from the biblical message, but rather a discerning call to 'Take, read' and more effectively minister God's word."

— KEVIN J. VANHOOZER
editor of *Dictionary for Theological
Interpretation of the Bible*

READING FOR PREACHING

The Preacher in Conversation with Storytellers,
Biographers, Poets, and Journalists

Cornelius Plantinga Jr.

WILLIAM B. EERDMANS PUBLISHING COMPANY

GRAND RAPIDS, MICHIGAN / CAMBRIDGE, U.K.

Published 2013 by
Wm. B. Eerdmans Publishing Co.
2140 Oak Industrial Drive N.E., Grand Rapids, Michigan 49505 /
P.O. Box 163, Cambridge CB3 9PU U.K.

Printed in the United States of America

19 18 17 16 15 14   7 6 5 4

Library of Congress Cataloging-in-Publication Data

Plantinga, Cornelius, 1946-
Reading for preaching : the preacher in conversation with storytellers,
biographers, poets, and journalists / Cornelius Plantinga, Jr.
        pages   cm
Includes bibliographical references.
ISBN 978-0-8028-7077-3 (pbk. : alk. paper)
1. Preaching.   2. Books and reading — Religious aspects — Christianity.
3. Christianity and literature.   I. Title.

BV4211.3.P64   2013
251 — dc23

                            2013020947

www.eerdmans.com

For Jack Roeda, dear friend,

who reads more voraciously and intelligently than anyone,

whose smart reading lights up his marvelous preaching, and

who, for decades now, has kept calling me up: "Neal, have you

read X? Have you read Y?" I'm trying to keep up with you, Jack.

I put the evidence in this book.

Contents

Preface

Preachers usually learn theology from theologians, and why not? Good theologians think hard about God and the world through all the mysteries of creation, fall, redemption, and consummation. Then they publish the fruit of their thinking, inviting us to gather as much of it as we want. Augustine, Anselm, Aquinas, Calvin, Schleiermacher, Barth, and a host of others offer preachers nourishment that a forty-year ministry will never consume. Who would ever outgrow Augustine on the heart's true home or Aquinas on the virtues? Who would have thought that the austere John Calvin could write as beautifully as he does on prayer or that Friedrich Schleiermacher, the father of liberal theology —and of *difficult* liberal theology — could preach the gospel simply and powerfully at the funeral of his son?[1] People praise the breadth and generative vision of Karl Barth's theology, but the preacher who merely looks up his weekly text in Barth's Scripture indexes will already be way ahead simply because Barth's imagination suggests possibilities that have dawned on nobody else.

The great theologians moreover encourage habits of lifetime learning. For example, they encourage preachers to get into the

---

1. Friedrich Schleiermacher, "Sermon at Nathanael's Grave," in *A Chorus of Witnesses,* ed. Thomas G. Long and Cornelius Plantinga Jr. (Grand Rapids: Eerdmans, 1994), pp. 256-61. The sermon begins, "My dear friends, come here to grieve with this stooped father at the grave of his beloved child."

interrogative mood and stay there a while. Can we hurt God? If not, how can God have compassion? If so, is God's interior life at our disposal? How can a virtue such as patience be both fruit of the Spirit and also our human calling? Why, besides its other victims, is sin a form of self-abuse? What, exactly, does God get out of the atoning sacrifice of Jesus Christ? If Jesus was truly sinless, if he never grieved over his treacheries or mourned his neglect of loved ones, can we still say that in him God was sharing our lot? How does petitionary prayer work and for whom? Why is grace sometimes more devastating than punishment?

Thoughtful preachers seek theological guidance in their shelves of old books, but also among their new ones. They have Anselm of Canterbury on "faith seeking understanding," but they also have Daniel Migliore of Princeton on it.[2] They mean to keep fresh water flowing in their theology. Like the faithful farmer Robert Frost describes, resourceful preachers are always out to "clean the pasture spring."[3]

In this mission theologians help the preacher immeasurably, but so do storytellers, biographers, poets, and journalists. Like theologians, they write about sin and grace, bondage and redemption, sorrow and joy, and the hunger for justice. A writer need not be a Christian to enlighten a Christian preacher. As John Calvin saw, the Holy Spirit sows truth promiscuously, and the searching preacher is likely to find it in some unlikely places.

Apart from its theological advantages, a program of general reading appeals to preachers for lots of reasons, one of which is sheer pleasure. There is a peculiar joy in entering an author's

2. Daniel L. Migliore, *Faith Seeking Understanding,* 2nd ed. (Grand Rapids: Eerdmans, 2004).

3. Frost, "The Pasture," in *The Poetry of Robert Frost: The Collected Poems,* ed. Edward Connery Lathem (New York: Henry Holt, 1969), p. 1. My friend and colleague W. Hulitt Gloer has pointed me to this image.

world, dwelling in it for a time, and coming to love it enough that you grieve when it is time to leave. If preachers enter the world of Harry Potter they will find their imagination stirred, which is another advantage of their reading program. What if in our preacher's sermons owls start to deliver mail once in a while? What if Voldemort looms up out of the darkness, or what if the Weasleys spread some of their family warmth? Our preacher will make fast friends of most 13-year-olds in the congregation and therefore of their parents and grandparents.

In this book I want to present the advantages to the preacher of a program of general reading. Good reading generates delight, and the preacher should enjoy it without guilt. Delight is a part of God's shalom and the preacher who enters the world of delight goes with God.

But storytellers, biographers, poets, and journalists can do so much more for the preacher. Good reading can tune the preacher's ear for language, which is her first tool. A preacher who absorbs one poem a day (perhaps from Garrison Keillor's *The Writer's Almanac*)[4] will tune his ear, strengthen his diction, and stock his pond with fresh, fresh images. That's before breakfast: after it, there's a day's worth of rumination on whatever the poet has seen of the human condition.

General reading can, moreover, provide the preacher with some of the choicest sermon illustrations in the land, and especially as a fruit of the preacher's practiced attentiveness to everything going on around him, whether or not printed on a page. Illustrations can be tricky, as we shall see, and reading expressly for them is probably not such a good idea. Nonetheless, the alert preacher is likely to come away from a stirring piece of writing with some things striking enough to save for the day he will need them.

4. http://writersalmanac.publicradio.org/.

Above all, the preacher who reads widely has a chance to become wise. Few people grasp the preacher's challenge. Where else in life does a person have to stand weekly before a mixed audience and speak to them engagingly on the mightiest topics known to humankind — God, life, death, sin, grace, love, hatred, hope, despair, and the passion and resurrection of Jesus Christ? Who is even close to being adequate for this challenge?

Nobody, and yet the preachers who accept the challenge have an opportunity to learn wisdom on the great topics from some of the most thoughtful writers God ever created.

One day in 2002 I was in a conversation with two colleagues at Calvin College — Susan Felch and John Witvliet — who proposed something that ended up changing my life.[5] They proposed that the next year I should offer a seminar in the Summer Seminars program at Calvin (which Susan directed at the time) and that its topic should be Reading for Preaching.

The idea immediately grabbed me. I had been convinced for decades that next to knowledge of Scripture and of the topics in a seminary curriculum, a preacher is extremely likely to benefit from a program of general reading, including of stories, biographies, poems, articles, and much else. Of course a preacher can often discover illustrations in these sources, and anyone familiar with the preaching of, say, Tim Keller or Fleming Rutledge or John Buchanan knows how nifty their illustrations can be. But reading just for illustrations feels a little too much like work. It also feels as if I am missing the point of reading, just as if I read the Bible only to see what it has to say about the colors green and red. I want to be reading stories and articles for nobler reasons while

5. Susan Felch is Professor of English at Calvin College and Director of the Calvin Center for Christian Scholarship. John Witvliet is Director of the Calvin Institute of Christian Worship and Professor of Worship, Theology, & Congregational and Ministry Studies at Calvin College and Calvin Theological Seminary.

an incident or insight or saying rises up from the page and begs to slip into one of my sermons.

More on those nobler reasons later.

In the summer of 2003 the pioneer edition of the Summer Seminars in Reading for Preaching brought twenty preachers to Calvin's campus for four weeks. We read John Steinbeck's *The Grapes of Wrath*, following Ma Joad and her brood out to the central valley of California, a valley of fading dreams and of sinking hearts. We read Robert Caro on the Senate years of Lyndon Baines Johnson, pondering how it happened that from 1949 to 1956 Johnson used his bag of tricks to block every piece of civil rights legislation that came before the United States Senate and then, in 1957, used all the same tricks to pass the first piece of civil rights legislation in over eighty years.[6] We used Anne Lamott's *Traveling Mercies* to enter her world, the Land of Lamott, a place in which even smallish things are wonderfully off kilter.

One day Susan Felch came to visit us. She came to turn off our alarms where poetry is concerned and to explore the power and beauty within the poetry of Robert Frost and Jane Kenyon. She taught us that poets are like preachers: they study how to say a lot in few words.

One day Gary Schmidt came to visit us. His purpose was to introduce us to the delights of great children's literature. Gary is another Calvin College English professor and an award-winning author of young people's fiction. There we sat, a group of mostly male middle-aged preachers, each with a children's book in hand, starting to look like children ourselves as we saw more deeply into our books and grasped the wonders in them. Gary reminded us that books written for children are never written only for

---

6. Robert Caro, *Master of the Senate*, vol. 3 of *The Years of Lyndon Johnson* (New York: Knopf, 2002), pp. 868-70.

them. As J. R. R. Tolkien saw, such books are written for the child-like, for the kind of people Jesus prized.

Every year since 2003 I have led seminars in Reading for Preaching with W. Hulitt Gloer, my colleague from Baylor University, or else with Scott Hoezee, my colleague from Calvin Theological Seminary — both of whom were in the original seminar of 2003.[7] The three of us have by now sat with many hundreds of seminary students and preachers from all over North America. We sit to read and then to consider why a preacher wants to do it.

The seminars have changed my life. Nothing in over thirty years of theological education has given me the joy of watching preachers discover the wonders within general literature and then imagine how to strengthen their preaching with them. Nothing has taught me more about the common grace of God than the fact that a lot of the wonders have been written into their books by people who do not know God.

In 2012 I gave the Warfield Lectures at my Ph.D. alma mater, Princeton Theological Seminary. President Ian Torrance, faculty members, including my beloved teacher and friend Daniel Migliore, students, staff members — all were wonderfully hospitable to my wife Kathleen and me, and I am deeply grateful to them. Like this book, the lectures were titled Reading for Preaching: The Preacher in Conversation with Storytellers, Biographers, Poets, and Journalists. For four nights and days in Princeton I tried to sell the students and professors on the benefit of reading for preaching. Judging by their response, I think they bought it.

7. Hulitt is the David E. Garland Professor of Preaching and Christian Scriptures, Director of the Kyle Lake Center for Effective Preaching, and Visiting Professor of Law, Baylor Law School. Scott is Director of the Center for Excellence in Preaching at Calvin Theological Seminary. Both men are gifted preachers and teachers of preaching. Both have taught me a great deal about reading for preaching.

I have adapted the Warfield Lectures for this little book just because I want to invite you to join the conversation with great writers. Doing so might change your life.

Christian preachers today are both men and women; accordingly I will alternate by chapter in my use of masculine and feminine pronouns for preachers.

Chapter 1

Introduction to the Conversation

Let's say that preaching is the presentation of God's Word at a particular time to particular people by someone the church authorizes to do it. God's Word in a sermon addresses people at many different levels and in many different times and seasons. But in every season Christian preaching centers where Christians think the Bible centers, namely on the reconciling work of Jesus Christ our Lord, especially through his death and resurrection.

Important questions cluster here including a central one: Does a Christian minister preach a text or preach the gospel? Suppose a text he's considering doesn't seem initially to have much gospel in it. It's a warning about what God will do to the wicked. Or it's a genealogy that seemingly ends in a historical cul-de-sac. It's a zoological tour in Job or it's a ripe old piece of wisdom: "Train up a child in the way he should go, and when he is old he will not depart from it." That is the KJV of Proverbs 22:6 and for many generations of English-speaking believers it was a charter for parental discipline.

Preach a text or preach the gospel? Preach a sermon that could as easily have been preached in a synagogue? Or find the gospel somewhere in Proverbs 22:6, even though it doesn't seem to be there? Or skip Proverbs 22:6? Or convert to Marcionism and skip the Old Testament altogether? Or what?

Here, of course, is where the Revised Common Lectionary

can help the preacher in lots of instances, though in the case of Proverbs 22:6 the Lectionary detours right around it, listing only verses 1-2 and 8-9 for Proper 18 in Year B. So the preacher who wants to address this famous text might have to find his own gospel and epistle pairings for it. And he might end up pondering with his congregation that kindness and laughter in a home are generationally as contagious as abuse, and that they provide acoustics in which the gospel of grace will sound plausible and resonant, even to the children of preachers.

Preach a text or preach the gospel? Either way, I'm assuming that preachers are addressed by God's Word just as much as the rest of us and that the power of a good sermon derives in part from its authenticity in this way. The preacher is not just a speaker of God's Word, but also a hearer, and a hearer before he is a speaker. That's why we can sometimes detect a sense of anticipation in our preacher as he reads Scripture in preparation for the morning sermon. He has a good idea of what God might be about to say.

Authentic preaching is personally committed preaching. The church's pulpit is never disinterested because the preacher, like the rest of us, has a stake in the truth of the gospel. In fact, the sermon's message ultimately comes only through, and not from, the preacher and it centers on the same God who sends it. "For we do not proclaim ourselves," as St. Paul put it; "we proclaim Jesus Christ as Lord" (2 Cor. 4:5).

Jesus Christ is the center, but there are lots of routes to the center in a good program of preaching, and they depend naturally on the text of the day and especially on what the text does.

Doing and Saying

Classically speaking, to preach a text is to do in other words what the text does. So, depending on the text, the preacher might inform people one Sunday and challenge them the next. He might praise, or lament, or reassure, and if he preaches the gospel he often reassures. If he has hold of a wise text he might counsel us from the pulpit. A faithful preacher will sometimes provoke us if his text is provocative enough. If his text is in the interrogative mood, maybe our preacher will follow suit by turning a big part of the sermon into a repeated question. "Who proved to be neighbor to this man?" "Lord, why are you so far away?" "Are you the one who is to come, or are we to wait for another?"

In any case, the preacher's job is not just to repeat a text, but also to outfit it for the hearing of a congregation. The preacher not only does in other words what the text does. He also says in other words what the text says, dressing it up or down, shaping and coloring and amplifying it in such a way that when people hear the preached text they hear God's word to them.

Here the preacher's use of illustrative material comes into play and here is the most obvious place where a congregation meets the preacher's conquests in the field of reading. Whether the preacher quotes writers, paraphrases them, summarizes them, or merely alludes to them, this is how Flannery O'Conner shows up in a Sunday sermon, or William Manchester, the great biographer of Winston Churchill, or Jane Kenyon, a poet of heartbreaking poignancy, or a Pulitzer Prize–winning newspaper series by Clifford J. Levy and Ellen Barry on the impenetrable corruption of Russian public life and the violent suppression of journalists who report it.[1]

1. http://www.pulitzer.org/citation/2011-International-Reporting.

Pretty Sermons?

Almost from the start you might wonder whether we *want* preachers to be in conversation with the likes of poets and storytellers. Won't this make preachers sound too lush for ordinary people? Preachers start conversing with poets and maybe lose their common touch. Their sermons start filling with allusions to literature in the manner, let's say, of some of the American pulpit giants of the 1930s and 1940s. One of them, the New York preacher Paul Scherer would begin a sermon like this: "Synge once said, with cutting cynicism, that Life is a table-d'hote in a rather dirty restaurant, with Time changing the plates before you have had enough to eat."[2]

But who is Synge? Scherer assumed people knew the Irish playwright and poet John Millington Synge and that it was enough to refer to Synge by last name alone. In the same sermon Scherer refers to "Mr. Dreiser and Mr. Mencken and Mr. Shaw," assuming that these, too, are household names.

If preachers converse with storytellers and poets won't we get literary sermons that assume congregational knowledge of such literary types as Irish poets and playwrights? And once our preacher starts conversing with poets, what stops him from quoting them? What if our preacher quotes from the *The Rubaiyat* of Omar Khayyam?

> Ah Love! Could you and I with fate conspire
> To grasp this sorry state of things entire,
> Would not we shatter it to bits — and then
> Remould it nearer to the heart's desire.[3]

---

2. Paul Scherer, "This Tired World," in his *The Place Where Thou Standest* (New York: Harper, 1942), p. 3.

3. http://www.youtube.com/watch?v=531R4W48ggo.

Before he started conversing with Khayyam, our plain-spoken preacher would say to us, "Wouldn't you like to make life go the way you want?" Now he says, "Ah Love! Could you and I with fate conspire. . . ." Once upon a time our preacher would say that the women came to Jesus' tomb early in the morning. But now he says that the women came to the tomb just as "the dawn was blushing pink behind the hills of Moab." He's been reading poetry and the sermons of Peter Marshall and they have taken him out where the rest of us do not go.

I believe our enthusiasm for his journey would be mild.

So let me say at the outset that in recommending a program of general reading for preachers I will not be asking for a recrudescence of what Reinhold Niebuhr called "pretty sermons." Niebuhr appears to have had in mind not just poetry-laden sermons, or florid sermons, but any sermons of highly refined rhetoric. Niebuhr said he wanted to keep his sermons "rough," instead, "just to escape the temptation of degenerating into an elocutionist."[4] Writing in his diary in Detroit, Niebuhr recorded some of the hard edges of the labor and racial issues he saw every day. No wonder he had little use for high rhetorical art in the pulpit. It must have seemed to him wholly irrelevant to his context.

I take Niebuhr's point and am grateful for it. This should not, in my judgment, silence preachers who sometimes quote fiction or who can turn phrases of their own when necessary. Everything depends on whether the quotations and phrases serve to make the gospel of grace sound more urgently alive or whether they serve merely to make the sermon more aesthetically pleasing. When the sermon is over, does the preacher want hearers to say "Thanks be to God!" or "How lovely that was, really"?

---

4. Reinhold Niebuhr, *Leaves from the Notebook of a Tamed Cynic* (New York: World Publishing, 1957; reprint of 1929 ed.), p. 27.

In recommending reading for preaching, my interest is not particularly aesthetic. I am as blessed as anyone by listening to a lovely sermon once in a while, especially when it is an expansion of a lovely text such as Psalm 103. But my agenda here lies elsewhere. I am convinced that the preacher whose work is supported by wide exposure to great writing will be significantly improved by it, including in the ways I mentioned in the Preface. Here I will add two more ways. The reading preacher will discover that great writers know the road to the human heart and, once at their destination, know how to move our hearts. To the preacher, knowledge of what stirs human hearts is golden and not at all because heart stirring is a good project all by itself. After all, some hearts can be stirred by masochistic sex or sentimental dreck. No, the preacher wants his heart stirred because he will then have some idea how the power and beauty of the gospel might be presented so that the hearts of his brothers and sisters may also be moved.

Bridging the Gap

Further, writers know their way around the world. They may enlarge the preacher's sympathies for people and situations he had previously known nothing about. If I am a parochial West Michigan Calvinist (Calvinists in cloudy West Michigan basically know how to experience gloom and how to cause it) I want authors to take me away. As citizens of the Kingdom of God that embraces people of "every nation . . . all tribes and peoples and languages" (Rev. 7:9), preachers want their reading to help bridge the circumstantial gap between themselves and people whose lives may otherwise be unfamiliar. As Adrian Piper writes in a discerning essay, if you say as a man that you cannot imagine what it would be like for a woman to be raped, or that as a white person in a majority white culture you cannot imagine what it's like to be racially taunted, then maybe you are humble and realistic. Maybe you know the presumption expressed by anything in the neighborhood of "I know just how you feel."

On the other hand, maybe your ignorance is due only to a cool lack of interest. Maybe you do not care to read literature, view paintings, listen to requiems, or partake of any other "literary and artistic products designed precisely to instruct us" about the exigencies of lives other than our own. Ignorance of the literary and fine arts is thus a serious sin of omission.[5] If so, perhaps purgatory, in a fine blending of judgment and grace, will include massive remedial instruction in the arts. The point is that identification with others may be partly instinctive, but it is also partly deliberate — and thus dependent upon an educated attempt to stretch our sympathies across circumstantial distance.

Think in this connection of a novel like Shusaku Endo's *Silence*,[6] which asks whether, under the pressure of sin, love can take unthinkable forms – ones that look a lot like betrayal. In the course of raising this question, the novel takes us to sixteenth-century Japan, giving us a feel not only for the Christian mission there and the ingenuity of its persecutors, but also for the Japanese suspicion that Christianity is less a religion than a means of Western cultural imperialism.

Or, consider Khaled Hosseini's *The Kite Runner*,[7] a tightly plotted first-person novel that explores the consequences for children of the sins of their fathers. The theme is universal but the setting is particular: most of the story transpires in contemporary Kabul. As

5. Adrian M. S. Piper, "Impartiality, Compassion, and Modal Imagination," *Ethics* 101 (1991): 739.

6. Endo, *Silence*, trans. William Johnson (New York: Taplinger, 1980).

7. Hosseini, *The Kite Runner* (New York: Riverhead, 2003).

a result the reader gets not only a cracking good story, but also exposure to Afghan culture — to food and drink, male and female relationships, Mullahs, kite-flying contests, tribal and intra-Muslim struggles between Pashtun Sunnis and Hasara Shias, and the daily threat of the Taliban. At one point the narrator, 12 years old at the start, reveals how dazed he was to discover that the American movies he had seen were dubbed, and that John Wayne didn't really speak Farsi and wasn't actually Iranian.

Great writers stretch our sympathies. In *Enrique's Journey* Sonia Nazario tells of the thousands of Central American children and teens who migrate north through Mexico each year in hope of reaching the United States and of being reunited with their loved ones. She tells in particular the story of Enrique, a boy from Tegucigalpa, whose father had left the family derelict and whose mother then had to face a cruel dilemma: she could stay with her family and watch her children go hungry or she could migrate to the U.S., get a job, and send money home. She left when Enrique was only five and, across the years, faithfully fulfilled her mission of supporting her children from abroad. After twelve years of this program, Enrique finally decided he couldn't bear to be without his mother, packed up some meager belongings, and began a 1,600-mile odyssey in trucks, buses, and, especially, on the tops of dangerous freight trains. After numerous failed attempts, he finally arrived at Nuevo Laredo, where a "coyote" hired by his mother smuggled him across the Rio Grande and into the promised land.

To authenticate her story of Enrique's journey, Nazario duplicated it, riding on swaying boxcars and facing all the same threats as the migrants did — of heat, cold, assault, robbery, rape, and accidental mutilation. She tells, as had Steinbeck in *The Grapes of Wrath*, of the community that forms among migrants who travel together: they share information, clothing, warnings of hazards, and what little food they can beg or buy. She tells of the sexual predators who see migrating girls as their natural prey (what else are they for?) and of kind-hearted local padres and residents who have little themselves, and yet give it to migrant strangers. Nazario offers no easy answers to the immigration challenge that the U.S. faces on its southern border, but her stellar journalism pretty much ensures that her readers will never again look at migrants in the same way.

Our Book

In recommending to preachers a program of general reading, I do not mean to underestimate the Christian preacher's first allegiance, which is to Scripture in two testaments. The Bible, as somebody's snooty bibliography will assure us, is "an older resource, but still valuable." In fact, Scripture is the church's endowment, the source along with the work of the Holy Spirit of the church's spiritual and emotional funding. To recall an image of John Calvin, the preacher is someone the church sends to the Bible week by week to dig up part of its treasure and bring it to us in the Sunday sermon.

The preacher is, first, an absorbed reader of the Bible and a champion of it among us. But because this role is so familiar it's easy for preachers to take it for granted. I was reminded of this several years ago. I was visiting on death row in the Louisiana State Penitentiary at Angola. I asked one man if he would like to talk, and he said he would. He's a smallish, African-American man whose wire-rimmed glasses and intelligent expression make him look a little professorial. I asked him how he spends his days. He picked up his NIV, hefted it, and said, "I spend a lot of time reading our book. I'm glad it's so big. I'll never get to the bottom of it." Then he said something I'll never forget. "You know," he said, "there are 2 billion of us Christians in the world, and everything today that any of us does that's any good has something to do with our book. And I have a copy of it right here in my cell!"

I came away from the visit with two powerful convictions. One was that I had almost certainly been underestimating our book. The other was that the idea of the state of Louisiana intending to kill this smallish lover of the Bible was appalling.

The preacher's first loyalty is to our community book, and nothing I write about a program of general reading supplants this in any way. The same goes for commentaries and other Scripture studies, which are the preacher's friends and which are the preacher's *dear* friends when they give evidence that the writer of the Scripture study has a feel for how certain passages might preach. I have in mind Ellen Davis, for example, and Thomas G. Long, of course, and Frederick Dale Bruner on Matthew and John, and Beverly Gaventa and William Willimon and many of the preacher's other dear friends.

Virtues of Short Fiction

The preacher's daily bread is Scripture and Scripture scholars. When theologians, ethicists, historians of the church, Christian philosophers, and experts in ministry gather in the preacher's life and mind as well, then his seminary education and continuing education will have done their job and I want nothing I write to distract from this blessed fact. But beyond it I want to recommend to preachers a program of more general reading to support ministry. I have novels in mind, of course, and will discuss passages from the likes of *Les Miserables* and *The Grapes of Wrath* in later chapters. But I'm thinking also of short stories which, besides their other virtues, are sometimes about the same length as a sermon, and can therefore show preachers compelling examples of a narrative arc in twenty-five hundred words. Amy Hempel can do it in half that length.

A big piece of sermon design has to do with how to start a sermon, how to stop one, how to introduce tension, how, and when, and whether to resolve it. These are staples of the preacher's craft, and short story writers work with these staples all the time and often to marvelous effect.

Let me add a practical note for busy preachers. Some great authors of novels also wrote short stories. This is true of Graham Greene, for example, a Brit, and of F. Scott Fitzgerald, an American. If you want Russian genius in smallish doses, and without your list of hard Russian names to keep straight, there is nothing like the stories of Tolstoy and Dostoevsky to light your fire on a frosty night. You have fewer names, fewer digressions and repetitions — just pure distillate of genius.

A number of these stories present issues and situations at the heart of the preacher's interest. Dostoevsky's novella "Notes from the Underground" is as psychologically acute on such things as human motives and free will as anything we can read in fiction. Then there is Tolstoy, as good a storyteller as God ever made, and an expert on the human heart.

In a story he composed in 1886 Tolstoy gives us a man named Pahom who loved land. He loved land more than anything and trusted it for his salvation. "If I had plenty of land," he says, "I shouldn't fear the Devil himself."[8] The Devil overhears him and arranges land-buying opportunities to start popping up for Pahom, including a big one.

---

8. Leo Tolstoy, "How Much Land Does a Man Need?" http://www.online-literature.com/tolstoy/2738/, I.

Pahom meets the Bashkirs, who are simple people with enormous resources of land. Pahom is delighted with their simplicity and figures it will come in handy. How could they know as much as he does about land purchase?

He is all the more delighted when he discovers their terms. For a flat rate of 1,000 rubles Pahom may keep as much land as he can circle on foot in a single day, sunrise to sunset. But if he does not get back to home base by sunset, he may keep none of the land and he forfeits the purchase price.

Pahom sets out on his day-long loop, marking his progress with a spade, but each time he thinks to start closing the loop he sees yet another grassy plain or sparkling stream or noble stand of trees, and he's got to have them. All of them. The loop keeps expanding till the shadows lengthen over it and Pahom realizes he's a long way from home base, and it's almost sunset. In a panic, Pahom starts dashing for the finish line. It's the longest and fastest he has ever had to sprint, but it is for the love of his life.

And he makes it! He reaches home base just as the last of the golden orb in the West disappears below the horizon. The Bashkirs all cheer and congratulate Pahom on his splendid achievement, but Pahom cannot hear them because he has dropped dead of a heart attack.

His servant buries Pahom in a box and the story ends. Tolstoy titled it "How Much Land Does a Man Need?" and he let Pahom's servant answer the question with a six-foot box, giving the preacher a six-foot image of the deadly sin of greed.

While we are in the Russian department — or, rather, the Russian/American department — the stories of Vladimir Nabokov come to mind. Many people know Nabokov only as the author of his novel *Lolita,* but in fact he wrote seventeen novels and also drama and literary criticism and biography. For a busy preacher, it is hard to beat Nabokov's short stories — many of them very short stories. Nabokov has wit and irony and poignancy to burn, and he wrote his later stories in English. He wrote stories in his second language with a grace and clarity most of us lack in our first.

One of his stories, titled simply "The Word," is about a barefoot and homesick man who finds himself surrounded in Paradise by turquoise birds, lithe orange animals, and a swarm of angels. When the angels can't restrain their bliss they unfurl their wings, and the sight is "like a burst of sunlight, like the sparkling of millions of eyes."[9]

Eventually the angels are called to a feast and recede, all but one. One angel stays, approaches the man, and embraces him with its wings for just an instant, just long enough to give the man a single word in which the man hears all the "beloved" and "silenced voices" of his homeland. The word is so fragrant and melodious that it spreads through the man like a drug, beating in his temples and spreading warmth in him such as he has never felt before.

If I am a preacher, I need not know what the angel's word was. But I do need to know that a word like this is possible, because angels speak for God.

Biographies, Journalism, Poetry

Fiction deepens the preacher, and so do biographies, which can usefully complicate our understanding of human character. David McCullough's biography of President Harry Truman comes to mind. McCullough tells us that Truman was backed by partly corrupt politicians, but that he was not corrupt. He was honest. But he was loyal to corrupt people and called them his friends. And the

9. http://www.newyorker.com/archive/2005/12/26/051226fi_fiction2?current Page=all.

preacher, always on the prowl, takes note for the day he will preach Jesus and Zaccheus. Maybe he will refer to Truman, and maybe not, but McCullough has equipped him to speak of Jesus as the friend of sinners with an authority he might not have felt before.

The preacher can profit from reading storytellers and biographers. But also journalists and essayists. An essayist of the quality of, say, Theodore Dalrymple or Joseph Epstein can help preachers see more deeply into biblical topics they handle every week. Guided by the principle of first things first, the honest preacher will let his exegeted text steer him through the sermon, not Dalrymple or Epstein, no matter how juicy their essays.

Still, suppose I am preaching on one of the biblical warnings against human self-importance. They are all over the place in Scripture, and not just in Proverbs. Here the gospel appears as a blessed relief from self-importance and from all its confounded anxieties and neuroses. Getting a sermon ready on self-importance and on grace that relieves it makes me want to become a minor expert on self-importance.

So, going in, I will want to be armed with Theodore Dalrymple's essay on the difference between self-esteem and self-respect.[10] Why have so many of us come to see high self-esteem as a Constitutional right, and why do we talk comparatively less often about the more disciplined trait of self-respect?

As I get my sermon ready, I'm brushing up on self-importance, and so, beyond Dalrymple, I read Joseph Epstein on the delicate art of name-dropping.[11] Name-dropping is the self-important person's low-budget advertising business.

A good drop, says Epstein, has to be at least plausible, even

10. Theodore Dalrymple, "Self-Esteem vs. Self-Respect," http://incharacter.org/features/theodore-dalrymple-on-self-esteem-vs-self-respect/.

11. Joseph Epstein, "Narcissus Leaves the Pool," in his *Narcissus Leaves the Pool: Familiar Essays* (Houghton Mifflin, 1999), pp. 1-20.

if it's false. At a dinner party you forfeit plausibility if your drop not only isn't true, but could not possibly be true. Suppose, in Epstein's example, that at a dinner party you pause to congratulate the table. "Wow," you say, "isn't this discussion terrific? Reminds me so much of the one I had last November when I lunched on Crete with Yo-Yo Ma and Dennis Rodman."

The preacher may profit from reading storytellers, biographers, and journalists. And from poets, too, but not primarily for pulpit quotation. Most audiences are not trained to listen to poetry from outside the Bible, and will not readily grasp it on a single hearing. And, frankly, some listeners cannot shake a populist suspicion of poetry: Isn't it too delicate a perfume?

Still, poets can help the preacher master his language. Nobody pays more attention to diction, rhythm, and euphony than a poet, and so the preacher, reading and reciting poetry behind closed doors, has much to gain. Poets may revise thirty or forty times in search of a precise beginning or ending, a staccato rhythm to match the topic, or a perfectly soft or hard word to finish a line. Perhaps above all, the revising poet is trying for economy, wanting to say a great deal in just a few words. Madeleine L'Engle describes the goal here: "The good writer will always limit herself. The simplest word is almost always the right word. . . . One of my favorite authors, Anon, wrote, centuries ago:

> The written word
> Should be clean as bone,
> Clear as light,
> Firm as stone.
> Two words are not
> As good as one.[12]

12. L'Engle, *A Circle of Quiet* (New York: Seabury, 1972), pp. 148-49.

The preacher will gain substance from his conversation with storytellers, biographers, poets, and journalists. Obviously, I mention these four groups only as important samples of the riches available to preachers. There are others. Memoirs, for instance, which are species of autobiography. Cultural criticism. Psychological studies. General history. Topical history. Travel writing. Film criticism. Whatever it is that Anne LaMott writes.

Web Media and Visual Media

And then, of course, there are all the web media, including the social media such as Facebook and Twitter, and the more intellectual web media, including terrific blogs by people who write knowledgeably about their specialties. I have in mind, for example, Juan Cole of the University of Michigan, who's a public intellectual and historian of the Middle East. With his weblog titled "Informed Comment" he's become one of the real luminaries of the intellectual blogosphere. He's all the more stimulating because his very definite point of view on the Middle East is controversial.

We may add the more conventional popular media to the preacher's resources, including films and TV, which many congregations will know better than books so that, as a preacher, I will feel pressure to stay reasonably current with what my congregation is viewing. There is wealth for preachers in TV and films. Admittedly, few films and TV programs use language as exquisitely as the best fiction and biographies, but they do deliver on some of the other benefits of reading — providing illustrations, for instance, and stimulating the preacher's imagination, and tending to make him wise.

Used as illustrations, video material can be compelling but

also tricky. If you show a video clip inside a sermon, and if it is powerful, it may overwhelm the rest of the sermon, and especially if the clip is so powerful that the appropriate response to it is silence. Film clips also need patient contextualizing to help the congregation understand them, just as surely as would a quote from Joyce Carol Oates.

Apart from actually showing clips, if you refer to a film within a sermon, you run up against a stubborn fact: films are visual media and visual effects are hard to describe. Films carry a lot of their freight in facial expressions and subtle body language or, more dramatically, in panoramic sweeps and spectacular action sequences. That is the nature of the medium. Can you describe the look of the Nazi officer in the film *Sophie's Choice* as he *gives* Sophie her choice? He tells her that he will kill one of her two children and that she must choose which. His face as he discloses this choice is as evil as any face I have ever seen in film and impossible to describe.

Films are a *visual* medium. This makes references to them dicey. The part of their package you can actually describe (what happens, what happens next, who said what) is not materially different from a short story, so then we're back on the familiar ground of character and plot and narrative movement.

Naturally, our well-read preacher will still need to do his exegetical and hermeneutical work honestly. He will still need to know his context and how to speak authentically within it. He will still need his mature sense of pastoral identity and all his leadership skills. Above all, he will need his life of faith and prayer, the only renewable resource that guards his integrity as a preacher and has at least a chance of preventing burnout.

But if he adds a reading program to all this, he enlists scores of helpers as he assembles the Sunday sermon. Authors are now at his side, joining him in the weekly challenge of meeting Sunday morning with confidence — scores of people to inform, persuade, inspire, and vivify his use of the English language.

A Superfluous Recommendation?

But, a question: Doesn't everybody already know that preachers ought to read a lot? In fact, don't preachers themselves know this with such conviction that they read novels all the time? Everybody knows preachers ought to be readers, and preachers know this too, so their weekly schedule is heavy with reading appointments. All of them are like this. Every single one of them. They picked up their good habits in college, where deep reading of classical canonical literature was a staple of their education in small classes with Ph.D. professors beaming over Dickens and George Eliot — professors who loved literature and passed on their love and joy to their students, and especially to their beloved pre-sems.

Well.

I will not waste your time in explaining why most of this ain't so. I will say only that for ten years I have co-hosted summer and winter seminars for preachers on reading for preaching, and that I have formed certain definite impressions on the topic. One of them is that we need not worry that a recommendation of reading for preaching is superfluous. Some preachers read storytellers and biographers. A very few read poets. Most do read various sources of journalism, especially in thin slices online. But as far as a solid program of general reading is concerned, there we are in more of an area for growth.

I will not claim that preachers who take up this program all become terrific preachers. Some do not. Maybe their innards are stony ground that cannot absorb a lot from their reading. Or maybe these preachers only flit amongst their books, never landing anywhere to pick up an actual treasure or two. Or maybe they actually amass quite a lot of treasure, but cannot manage it. They do not store and retrieve their riches very well and regularly sit in front of their computer tormented by a near certainty that they once read something good — in fact something *perfect* for right here in the sermon. But what was it?

It makes you wonder whether it is truly better to have read and lost than never to have read at all.

Or maybe the preacher gathers good things from his reading and tries to fatten his sermons with it, but then distracts listeners with quotes that do not quite fit, or with insights too subtle to be dropped without explanation into the Sunday morning sermon, or with too many insights coming too thick and fast. Suppose, for instance, that the morning's assignment is one of the shame texts from Scripture, one of the psalms, for example, that has gloating enemies in it. The preacher drops into the sermon Robert Karen's observation that shame is contagious, that when we are around somebody who is ashamed our own "shame demons" begin to stir.[13]

That is a significant insight with implications all over the place, including in family systems theory. It deserves elaboration. But what if the preacher doesn't elaborate the idea that shame is contagious but right away delivers another insight from Karen, namely, that we are often ashamed not only of our own deficiencies, but also of the deficiencies of others, and particularly when we think their deficiencies make us look bad. Then we are like the college student at the first parents' weekend who really doesn't want anybody to meet his unrefined mother.

That's a good insight too and it also deserves elaboration, but

13. Robert Karen, "Shame," www.leadercenter.ru/Shame_Robert_Karen .doc.

our preacher doesn't elaborate and keeps plowing ahead. He says we can catch shame from others and we can also *be* ashamed of others and, besides shame isn't quite the same thing as guilt, and besides . . . The treasures from our preacher's reading are flying at us and now everybody in the congregation is silently saying, "Hold it! Hold it! Slow down! What was that business about shame being a disease, or what was it?"

Too much too fast. I have found over the years that with seminary students one of the hardest things for them to believe is that they really needn't try to stuff everything but their backpack into a twenty-four minute sermon.

I do not claim that a program of general reading always turns the people who do it into terrific preachers. Much, much else is required, including empathy, charity, plain common sense, intelligence, and especially vital faith in the Lord of the gospel. Nor, on the other side of the street, do I claim that all terrific preachers are wide readers. In fact, a few non-reading preachers I know nonetheless appear to move their listeners in some of the central ways I most admire. I do not have in mind only preachers who know where to press the buttons in excitable hearers. No, I'm thinking of a few preachers who have natural insight into Scripture derived from years of reading and pondering it. They have natural insight into people derived from genuine empathy with them and curiosity about their lives. They pray persistently. They have built up stores of wisdom from years of close attention to life, perhaps from travel, perhaps from fascinating friends, perhaps from TV, certainly from their pastoral care. They have a deep and abiding sense of the presence of God, and a hunger for God's justice in the world, and a seemingly inexhaustible fascination with Jesus Christ today, yesterday, and forever. They have mastered whatever style of preaching their congregation thrives on and so they preach that way Sunday by passionate Sunday.

Because of where they minister, they do not need Russell Banks novels to tell them about blue-collar despair, with its busted screen doors and Chevy Impalas up on cinder blocks in the front yard. Because of who they are, they do not need Hemingway to tell them the sun also rises; they just look out the window. They could never tell you the difference between Julian Huxley and Aldous Huxley, and they don't care and neither does their happy congregation.

I do not claim that only wide readers can preach you a powerful Sunday sermon, and I do not claim that every wide reader will turn into a powerful preacher. My claim is more modest, namely this: especially for those of us without the greatest natural gifts and empathies, a program of general reading is very likely to improve us in excellent ways.

My aim here is to lay out some of those ways.

Chapter 2

Attentive Illustrations

Good writers typically supply a fair number of preachers' "illustrations," as we call them. The term is actually a catch-all for anecdotes, analogies, stories, blog entries, editorial opinions, famous tweets, incidents from history, memorable sayings, biographical profiles, statistics, snippets of dialogue from TV interviews, lines from Wikipedia bios, lines from poems, news reports, people's comments on news reports, summaries of film plots, sentences from one of Bonhoeffer's prison letters, and all the other fine things preachers gather, store, and retrieve in order to dress their exegeted text decently so that when Sunday morning comes the preacher's sermon may appear "clothed and in [its] right mind."[1]

Dig Up Your Own Stuff

I wrote in the preface that reading general literature just for illustrations is slightly perverse. I want to read for better reasons and especially to be deepened and expanded by my reading. Reading gives me more substance to bring to Christian life and to Chris-

---

1. The allusion is to one of the truly remarkable texts in the gospels. In Mark 5 Jesus heals a man wild with demons. Afterwards, when people saw "the demoniac sitting there clothed and in his right mind. . . . They were afraid. . . . Then they began to beg Jesus to leave their neighborhood" (Mark 5:15-17 NRSV).

tian preaching. The thoughtful preacher gets a little bigger each time she reads. But, yes, along the way she will also discover a story, an incident, a saying that is striking enough to belong in a future sermon. If the preacher is a persistent reader, she will discover illustrations that may turn out to be more than mere embellishments. If well chosen and well placed, illustrations can become serious business within a sermon. In any case, good illustrating requires a high degree of attentiveness in the preacher whether she illustrates from her own thought and experience or from her program of reading or from somewhere else.

"Somewhere else" might be sermonillustrations.com or sermonideas.net, where the harried preacher can find prefabricated possibilities. These have often passed their "sell by" date. Let's say our preacher plans to present contentment from Philippians 4 and wants an illustration of the folly of discontentment. Sermonillustrations.com offers up this:

A man became envious of his friends because they had larger and more luxurious homes. So he listed his house with a real estate firm, planning to sell it and to purchase a more impressive home. Shortly afterward, as he was reading the classified section of the newspaper, he saw an ad for a house that seemed just right. He promptly called the realtor and said, "A house described in today's paper is exactly what I'm looking for. I would like to go through it as soon as possible!" The agent asked him several questions about it and then replied, "But sir, that's your house you're describing."[2]

An implausible illustration, of course, but, halfway into it, also predictable, which is a discouraging mix for a sermon il-

2. http://www.sermonillustrations.com/a-z/c/contentment.htm.

lustration. Sermonillustrations.com lists the author of this little number, by the way, as "anonymous," and I understand.

Preaching websites do contain better illustrations, but the good ones have all been used by other preachers in the hunt so that the chance of finding a really fresh one is small. In any case, none of them rose naturally to the preacher's attention within her own observation of life or her own program of reading, so none has been discovered and then owned by the preacher herself.

Nothing Is Lost on Her, not even Earl

If our preacher does dig up her own stuff, either from observation of daily life or from reading, the same quality of attentiveness will be at work both times. When she's out and about, her radar is on. An alert preacher picks up on things around her, and maybe some of them show up in sermons. Every so often in a sermon she might say, "Have you ever noticed . . . ?" Or, she'll say, "I've been keeping an informal tally of the number of times people claim to . . ." Or, one day, she's preaching along about how all of us with children want them to grow, but we ache when they do. For lots of reasons we ache when they grow. One reason is that our children start to question the opinions they learned from us. Why do they do that? It's so unnecessary. Our opinions were fine just the way they were.

Children start at some point to think for themselves and parents get a little antsy about it. Let's say our preacher is going along about this and then she says, "The other day I was coming home from Chicago, and the flight attendant said, 'Be cautious when opening the overhead bins, as contents may have shifted' and it got me to thinking about when children come home from college, their heads stuffed with radically new ideas. I want to say to their parents, 'Mom, Dad, be cautious when opening the overhead bins, as contents may have shifted.'"

This is a preacher with sharp eyes and ears. She's like Richard Mouw, from whom I got this bit about the overhead bins. And if she is as sharp as Mouw she will come up with quite a few good illustrations. But if she also reads widely she will multiply the number of eyes and ears out there working for her, spotting remarkable things she can use in her sermons. Her attentiveness then becomes a filter inside her reading, sorting what "will preach" from what won't. What we listeners get is a wonderful back-and-forth: the preacher's attentiveness to life also lets her spot good things in her reading, and the writers she reads also increase her attentiveness to life.

Good preachers notice things around them. Part of what they pick up is just human, except that every person they meet bears the image of God, so nobody is really "just" human. Everybody has surprising depths. Our preacher is at a church gathering and talking with Brad, a macho teen whose bravado has got to be armor over a tenderness she had not known anything about. The bravado has got to be armor because as Brad describes something that happened to his younger brother, his chin starts to quiver almost imperceptibly. He doesn't notice, but our preacher does, and it makes her wonder what other loves and sensitivities Brad is trying to shield with his bravado.

A good preacher does not miss much. Her skill in reading life is as important to her as her skill in reading Scripture. She is watching a men's basketball game at the local college and starts wondering about something. She wonders why players descending from a thunderous dunk look not pleased but angry. Why would that be? They have just added points for their team and done it with great brio. Why do they look so upset?

Or she is mowing the grass one fine day and some fine thoughts are coming to her on some fine topics, including some high-quality spiritual topics. When she takes a break her neighbor Éarl walks over to chat. Earl is a fine and faithful man with an almost genius-level ability to be uninteresting. Earl could make a tornado sound boring. He will be describing his sister-in-law's brother's allergies, and just when by spontaneous combustion something interesting flares up in Earl, he will interrupt himself to put it out.

Our preacher is attentive, so she listens — not with irritation but with amazement at the extraordinary levels of boredom Earl has achieved. As he climbs higher and higher into them, she starts to find Earl *fascinating*. How can a single human being of finite capacity spread out a wasteland so vast? Maybe the ordinary layperson would grow impatient with Earl, but our preacher thanks God for him because sentence after sentence Earl is teaching her things about preaching she could not have gotten from a whole shelf of books. Especially, as she thinks about Earl and then about her sermons she keeps saying to herself, "Leave some things out! For heaven's sake, leave some things out!"

The preacher's attentiveness to life has its benefits, and one of them is sermon illustrations. Of course she maintains confidentiality. Of course she protects Brad and her neighbor Earl and everybody else God gives her to protect.

But she never forgets Brad's quivering chin or Earl's manful efforts to reach new summits, and her observations of them become residue in her experience. One day she will draw upon her experience for a sermon illustration generalized enough to protect Brad or Earl but dependent on them for the verve and authority of the illustration itself.

Maybe the poignancy of what she meets in a boy like Brad

sets her up to find it all over the place. So in the online edition of the newspaper, one day in September, she spots an ad in the section titled "Bargain Corner." Here is the ad:

WEDDING DRESS — Mori Lee, size 18, runs small, still has tags, never worn, Asking $50.[3]

Let's hope the prospective bride had discovered just in time that her fiancé was wrong for her and had broken the engagement. But what if her fiancé had called the wedding off? What if her wedding had been her dream? What if at last a man had claimed to love her? What if her purchase of her wedding gown had been sheer joy?

Size 18. Runs small. Never worn. Asking $50.

Attentiveness is the preacher's gift and calling, and she can build her capacity for it by reading some of the most attentive people in the world. She can also gather sermon illustrations from them that will help bring her sermon to life.

Buchanan, Willimon, Rutledge, and Jonker at Work

For twenty-six years at Fourth Presbyterian Church in Chicago, John Buchanan did this with a passion. There are practically no Buchanan sermons without quotations, paraphrases, summaries, or references to something Buchanan had read. One Sunday in 2007 Buchanan preached on the story of Jesus' first recorded miracle, his turning of water into wine in the village of Cana. The story reminded Buchanan of something Wendell Berry, poet and farmer, had written:

3. Bargain Corner, *Grand Rapids Press*, September 17, 2011.

Whoever really has considered the lilies of the field and the birds of the air and pondered the improbability of their existence will hardly balk at the turning of water into wine, which was, after all, a very small miracle. We forget the greater miracle and still continuing miracle by which water with soil and sunlight is turned into grapes.[4]

Buchanan's illustration sets Jesus' miracle within the amazing acts of God in creation. By doing so the illustration rekindles listeners' delight in the lilies of the field and the birds of the air and the grapes of the vine.

On a Sunday in 2008 Buchanan preached on the atoning and forgiving grace of God. He wanted to offset the mighty work of God by speaking of the un-mighty work of us mortals. To do so, Buchanan summarized the story Ian McEwan tells in his novel *Atonement* and in the film based on it. Briony, a 13-year-old girl, catches a glimpse of her older sister Cecilia in an emotionally charged encounter with Robbie, the son of one of the family's servants, and later reads an aggressive love letter Robbie has written to Cecilia, but not sent. He had written it only wishfully. When Briony's cousin Lola is raped, Briony concludes that Robbie must have done it and falsely claims to have seen his face, a claim that gets Robbie jailed and breaks Cecilia's heart.

As Briony matures she comes to understand the damaging thing she has done and attempts to atone for it, only to discover a terrible truth: you cannot give back the years that the locusts have eaten. Human attempts at atonement are so often partial and troubled.[5]

---

4. http://www.fourthchurch.org/sermons/2007/011407.html. The Berry quotation is from *The Art of the Commonplace: The Agrarian Essays of Wendell Berry* (Berkeley, CA: Counterpoint, 2003), p. 313.

5. http://www.fourthchurch.org/sermons/2008/021008.html.

On May 11 of the same year, Buchanan faced a preacher's challenge: Pentecost was on the same Sunday as Mother's Day. Buchanan is a Christian minister and a churchman. He wanted to preach Pentecost. But it was also Mother's Day and, said Buchanan, "no preacher with any sense at all would risk ignoring it. Every year someone calls and says, 'I'm bringing mother to church Sunday, so make it good. And she doesn't want to hear about gun control.'"

But where do you look for Mother's Day illustrations that are not sentimental or already on Mother's Day cards, or both? You look within the vast emotional resources of Garrison Keillor. It happened that Keillor had written an op ed for the *Chicago Tribune* earlier in the week. Many of Buchanan's church members would already have read it, but Buchanan used it anyway because a fine illustration, like a fine ballad, can be done more than once. The topic of the op ed was "Nobody Loves You Like Your Mama Does":

"She loves you," Keillor wrote. "You could come home with snakes tattooed on your face and she would still see the good in you. She knows when you're in trouble. And you will get into deep trouble someday. Count on it. But your mother will still love you. Like an old lioness, she'll come running, even if you're 2,000 miles away."[6]

Preachers dig up treasures from their reading in order to illuminate a biblical situation or person or idea. Perhaps, like Will Willimon on one Sunday in the Duke Chapel, the preacher has hold of one of those texts in the gospels in which Jesus resists the popular urge to blame victims of disasters. A tower falls on them, and everybody wants to say "They must have done *something!*"

6. http://www.fourthchurch.org/sermons/2008/051108.html.

Maybe, like Willimon, the preacher will cite Thornton Wilder, *The Bridge of San Luis Rey*.[7] This is an unsettling story about six South American villagers who fell to their deaths when the village bridge snapped. The local priest decided to find out why they, of all the villagers, had perished. What had they done? How had they sinned? He studied the lives of the six and, at the end of his study, concluded they had been no better and no worse than anybody else who had made it safely across.

"They must have done *something*." Apparently not.

On another Sunday, the text is from Romans 7, a chapter in which Paul describes the bondage of the will. He writes famously, "I do not do the good I want to do, but the evil I do not want to do — this I keep on doing." At one point our preacher mentions that when William Faulkner received the Nobel Prize for literature he stated that "the central human drama is the heart in conflict with itself." Our preacher brings Faulkner in to reinforce Paul.

Or maybe, on another Sunday, she enlists Shakespeare to comment on the text of the day from 1 Corinthians 15: "love never ends." Here is Shakespeare in Sonnet 116:

> Love is not love
> Which alters when it alteration finds . . .
> O no, it is an ever fixed mark
> That looks on tempests and is never shaken . . .

These last two examples are from Fleming Rutledge, who often illustrates from her wide reading and to memorable effect.[8]

---

7. William Willimon, "When Bad Things Happen to Good People," in *The Collected Sermons of William H. Willimon* (Louisville: Westminster John Knox, 2010), p. 64.

8. Rutledge, "Christ vs. Adam: Kosovo and Beyond" and "The Faces of Love," in her *Help My Unbelief* (Grand Rapids: Eerdmans, 2000), pp. 40, 64.

Sometimes her references are reinforcements, as in the case of the Faulkner and Shakespeare examples, but perhaps more often her references are foils — honest foils. She takes seriously the devastating things people say against the faith and especially when Freud says them. She treats the cultured despisers as people from whom we have to learn before we set them aside.

Occasionally a preacher wants no more from her reading than a single quotable line. Will Willimon preached powerfully on sin one day in April 1995, saying again and again that the human problem is human sin, our sin, my sin. He concluded like this: "So G. K. Chesterton, when asked to write a magazine article on 'What's Wrong with the Universe,' responded to the editor's request, 'What's Wrong with the Universe' with one sentence, '*I am.*'" [9]

So the preacher may draw upon her reading to shine a light on human sin and on the mystery of evil in the lives of good people. She may light up a creation miracle such as turning water into wine or a redemption miracle, such as Jesus' full atonement for the sin of the world — even if she has to do it by way of contrast with troubled human attempts to atone. She may reinforce a biblical claim such as that love never ends or she may quote people who hate religion. She will put them right in the sermon and let us think about what they have to say. Maybe the cultured despisers of religion have more to teach us on a given topic than some of our blessed brothers and sisters whose untroubled faith presents no challenge to us.

Illustrations do not have to be from Faulkner or Shakespeare or Thornton Wilder. They could be from Harry Potter or *People* magazine or the autobiography of Jerry Sandusky. They could be

---

9. William Willimon, "My Sin," in *The Collected Sermons of William H. Willimon*, p. 176.

from John Calvin, but also from Calvin and Hobbes or advertising copy from Calvin Klein.[10] They could be from anywhere.

One classical locus of illustrative material is, of course, in the introduction to the sermon. The idea is to set up the theme of the day's text. Get people in the mood to think about it.

On Thanksgiving Day, 2011, my pastor Peter Jonker preached a marvelous sermon on Psalm 65 with an introduction from the life of Seth MacFarlane, who had been on NPR's *Fresh Air* program with Terry Gross. MacFarlane is a cartoonist and comedian. He's the creator of the animated comedy show "The Family Guy," which my pastor called "arguably the most cynical show on television."

Terry Gross asked MacFarlane about 9/11. It seems that on that day of national tragedy MacFarlane had been booked on American Airlines Flight 11, Boston to LA, but he had arrived late at Logan airport and missed it. As we know, hijackers flew Flight 11 into the North Tower of the World Trade Center.

My preacher said, "MacFarlane should have been on that plane. He should have been dead at 29 years of age. But somehow, at the end of that terrible day, he found himself healthy and alive, still able to turn his face toward the sun."

Terry Gross asked the inevitable question: "After that narrow escape, do you think of the rest of your life as a gift?"

"No," said MacFarlane. "That experience didn't change me at all. It made no difference in the way I live my life. It made no difference in the way I look at things. It was just a coincidence."

And my preacher commented that MacFarlane had created "a missile defense system" against the threat of incoming grati-

---

10. In the late 1990s legal counsel for the Calvin Klein clothing company sent a stern letter to Calvin College telling the college to cease and desist using the name Calvin. The College declined.

tude — which might have lodged in his soul and changed him forever.

MacFarlane, "the Grinch who stole gratitude," perfectly set up what Peter Jonker had to say to us about how it is right and proper for us to give thanks to God at all times and in all places, and especially when our life has been spared.

On the other end of a sermon, our preacher can effectively summarize and conclude her message with an apt illustration. Suppose the text of the day has to do with the providence of God, always at work to make something out of unpromising materials and unpromising people. The preacher's thoughts turn to Lyndon Baines Johnson, and to Robert Caro's magnificent multivolume biography of him.

As a young school teacher in the hill country of Texas, Johnson showed a generous heart for his students at the "Mexican school" of Catulla. He saw their poverty, their hunger, their pain, and came to their side. He arrived at school early and stayed late. He toted sports equipment after school, visited in his students' hovels, took his students to heart. He was a compassionate teacher.[11]

But his ambition took him to the nation's House of Representatives and then to the Senate. Johnson came to the U.S. Senate in 1949 as the junior Senator from Texas. He then rose through the ranks, becoming his party's Assistant Leader, then its Leader. Finally, in 1955, when Democrats took over the Senate, he became Majority Leader — one of the most powerful in the history of the position.

According to Robert Caro, power was Johnson's food and drink. He liked to say, "I do understand power, whatever else may be said about me. I know where to look for it, and how to

11. Robert Caro, *Master of the Senate,* vol. 3 of *The Years of Lynden Johnson* (New York: Knopf, 2002), pp. 720-21.

use it."[12] One of the things Johnson understood about power was that it came not only from mastery of timing and parliamentary procedure, but also from mastery of the personal biographies of Senators. So Johnson learned his Senators. In a visit with Arthur Schlesinger, Johnson

> ran down the list: each man's strengths and weaknesses, who liked liquor too much, and who liked women, and how he had to know when to reach a senator at his own home and when at his mistress's, who was controlled by the big power company in his state, and . . . which senator responded to one argument and which senator to the other argument.[13]

Because much of the Senate's power lay in the bloc of conservative southern Democrats, Johnson had cultivated them for years. Especially in the early 1950s, he flattered them shamelessly, sometimes sitting on the floor so he could physically look up at them. Or he would fulsomely praise his own father and then, ten minutes later, say to a Senator, "You've been just like a Daddy to me."[14] Aware that the southern bloc could advance his career, Johnson used all the tricks in his bag to protect the bloc's positions, particularly on "states' rights." Drawing upon his intimate knowledge of Senators, he would lie, or flatter, or bully — whatever was necessary to win his way. He would lean his long frame over another Senator, grab his lapel, or his shoulder, or his tie with one large paw and jab the Senator's chest with the other. He manipulated the Senate's rules and other Senators' pride or fear; he threatened and cajoled and beseeched. He called in favors.

12. Caro, *Master of the Senate,* epigraph.
13. Caro, *Master of the Senate,* p. 834.
14. Caro, *Master of the Senate,* pp. 155-56.

From 1949 to 1956, using all his powers, Lyndon Johnson blocked every piece of civil rights legislation that came to the floor of the Senate.

But then in August of 1956, at the Democratic nominating convention in Chicago, Johnson came to be whispered about as a possible dark horse nominee for President. Warming to the possibility, Johnson caught presidential fever. He let his imagination take him to the White House, and was then devastated when the convention abandoned him as a "sectional" candidate because of his record on civil rights. He had "the scent of magnolias" on him, and it wrecked his hope of a presidential nomination.[15]

In the fall of 1956 Lyndon Johnson took counsel with himself. And in 1957, he opened his bag of tricks once again. He manipulated and threatened and beseeched and cajoled. He got his southern power base to believe that he was still with them while simultaneously working against them. He got one of the most powerful of them, Richard Russell of Georgia, to believe that only after conceding something to the civil rights movement could Johnson one day become President and protect the South from more vigorous legislation.[16] And then on August 29, Lyndon Johnson rammed through the Senate the Civil Rights Act of 1957, the nation's first civil rights bill in over eighty years. And, of course, riding his momentum, Johnson would later become the President who did more for civil rights in America than any other President of the twentieth century. His compassion and his ambition were running on parallel tracks at last.[17]

Our preacher's theme that day is that God is ever the master of irony, that God hits straight shots with crooked sticks, that

15. Caro, *Master of the Senate*, pp. 804-24.
16. Caro, *Master of the Senate*, pp. 868-70.
17. Caro, *Master of the Senate*, pp. 722-23.

God's providence is inscrutable. She could just say so in her sermon. But if she illustrates from the life of LBJ, she has a chance of bringing her theme home in a fascinating way.[18]

In good preaching, illustrative material can become so much more than adornment. The best of it is "sinew and bone," as I have heard Fred Craddock say. The good stuff is part of the sermon to such a degree that if you were to remove it, that part of the sermon would cave in.

Moving the Heart

Maybe this is especially so when the preacher chooses illustrative material for its emotional impact. The choice needs a pure heart. More than one preacher has figured out how to tell stories or anecdotes that move people and has ended up manipulating them in the process.

Still, abuse does not negate good use. Sermons would feel airy if they never touched us to the quick. But faithful preachers do not use illustrations to manipulate us. Their illustrations have theological warrant and especially when they inspire us to find God's purposes and make them our own.

"True religion," said Jonathan Edwards, "consists in great measure in . . . the fervent exercises of the heart."[19] Edwards meant that, at its core, true religion has to do not just with kindling our passions, but also with aiming them in the right direction. The world is full of good. The Godly person will say Yes to it

18. And this is true whether the preacher uses this fat illustration at the end of a 45-minute sermon, or summarizes for a shorter sermon, or handles the length of this remarkable story in some other way.

19. Edwards, *Religious Affections*, vol. 2 of *The Works of Jonathan Edwards*, ed. John E. Smith (New Haven: Yale University Press, 1959), p. 99.

with all her heart and then act accordingly. The world is also full of evil. The Godly person will say No to it with all her heart and then act accordingly. The world is full of the mixture of good and evil so that the Godly person sometimes needs the gift of discernment before she knows what to say or how to act.

In any event, true religion always begins from the central place in us where we "hate what is evil" and "hold fast to what is good" (Rom. 12:9). A sequence of hearty Yes's and No's lies at the center of true religion, said Edwards, and this is why we sing our praise instead of merely saying it. This is why we preach the word instead of simply reading it. This is why in the Lord's Supper we "eat and drink our God."[20] The reason is that these are ways God customarily uses to start human hearts.

So preachers expose themselves to John Steinbeck's *The Grapes of Wrath* not only for its insights or narrative movement or structural genius. They read to get moved by compassion and by a hunger for justice. Preachers follow Ma Joad's family to California because they know a simple fact: their preaching is meant by God to move human hearts and they have no hope of success in this mission unless they are vulnerable to being moved themselves.

So suppose the text du jour is one from Isaiah or Jeremiah or Ezekiel about how God's judgment can leave the land desolate, or a house desolate, or the people desolate. Wind has swept the land of its crops, the farm animals have been sold or wandered off, the cities have turned into ghost towns, and the houses have been forsaken. What is this like? Preachers in search of illustrations could wander through Detroit, Michigan, or some of the emptied out towns on the American prairie. Preachers could report on desolation from their own experience.

20. Edwards, *Religious Affections*, p. 115.

Or the preacher could read *The Grapes of Wrath,* which tells what happened when the banks pushed the sharecroppers off the land and the wind blew away the crops and auctioneers sold the animals and the houses were left behind.

What is it like for a house to be left behind? In one of his virtuoso inter-chapters, Steinbeck tells us:

> The weeds sprang up in front of the doorstep, where they had not been allowed and grass grew up through the porch boards. . . . Splits started up the sheathing from the rusted nails. . . . On a night the wind loosened a shingle and flipped it to the ground. The next wind pried into the hole where the shingle had been, lifted off three, and the next, a dozen. The wild cats crept in from the fields at night, but they did not mew at the doorstep any more. They moved like shadows of a cloud across the moon, into the rooms to hunt the mice. And on windy nights the doors banged, and the ragged curtains fluttered in the broken windows.[21]

Perhaps eight lines of desolation here are too many for the preacher to quote. Maybe she wants to paraphrase part of the passage or all of it, except for that last line: "On windy nights the doors banged, and the ragged curtains fluttered in the broken windows."

The preacher reads Steinbeck and she discovers in detail how abandoned houses break down. Maybe she could have gotten that much from reading *The Complete Idiot's Guide to Purchasing Foreclosed Houses,* but it would probably not count as great literature. The point of reading great literature about forsaken houses is that it makes you care about the people who used to

21. John Steinbeck, *The Grapes of Wrath* (New York: Penguin, 2002), pp. 116-17.

live in them. You *feel* the desolation and maybe your feeling has the texture of compassion.

If our preacher can get the congregation to see what desolation looks like, and to feel what desolation feels like, maybe her sermon on Psalm 137 becomes poignant. In Psalm 137 God's people are camped along the rivers of Babylon and they are weeping. They are humiliated and homesick. They know that back home their cities are ghost towns. The wind has swept the grass off the land, auctioneers have sold the animals, and in the houses of Jerusalem the doors are banging and the ragged curtains are fluttering in the broken windows.

"By the rivers of Babylon we sat down and wept when we remembered Zion."

Good Judgment, Please

The preacher who illustrates from her reading may quote or paraphrase or summarize, but in any case will face questions of judgment. Given her setting, how apt is her illustration? How fancy? How suitable for a mixed audience? If the illustration is violent, how much violence can you bring to the third graders in the congregation? If the illustration is from political culture, will she distract the folks whose blood warms whenever she mentions Sean Hannity or Rachel Maddow?

Preachers always face questions of judgment about illustrations, including how many of them to use in a given sermon. A preacher who loves to illustrate can get carried away and give us sermons so chock full of stories and anecdotes that it's hard for us to find the main thread. The sermon is all beads and no string. Sermons like that can tire people out.

Preachers also need good judgment about the size of illustrations. Big illustrations are big risks: they may overwhelm the rest of the sermon. Little illustrations, if snipped from their context in the literature, may puzzle listeners, and the preacher who attempts to rebuild the context for them will need time and skill.

Over everything the preacher needs good judgment. Suppose she is preaching the Prologue to the Fourth Gospel. Not to put too fine a point on it, this is high Bible. The Prologue gives us literature as glorious as any in Scripture, and our preacher wants to understand exactly what she is doing with it as she preaches. In particular, she wants to know how to interpret John's term *ho logos*. The Word. She studies the term's provenance in John: Is it Jewish or Hellenistic or a hybrid? Is the gospel referring to an actual metaphysical entity that it calls "the Word," perhaps a hypostasis of God's revelation that then becomes incarnate as Jesus? If so, would that interpretation count for Jesus' pre-existence or against it? And what does all this mean for the doctrine of the Trinity?

After much study, our preacher concludes that maybe already in verse 1, but certainly some time later in the Prologue, "the Word" functions as a straight metaphor for Jesus. Jesus is "the Word." It's like calling him "the true light." It's like calling him "the Way," or "the Truth," or "the Life" — or "the bread of life." So, similarly, Jesus speaks for God the Father to such a remarkable degree that John can call him, simply, "The Word." After all, Jesus only says what he hears his Father saying.

Now the week has reached Thursday noon and our preacher is wondering how to bring this famous metaphor home for the congregation. On coffee break our preacher is knocking around Amazon.com and comes upon an ad for the 45th anniversary album of Frank Sinatra's song "My Way." She doesn't really know anything about Sinatra, but her parents used to talk about him, so she looks Sinatra up on Wikipedia, and then it hits her. She has her connection.

In 1946 America's then most popular singer cut his first album. It was called "The Voice of Frank Sinatra." From then on, Sinatra was often called simply The Voice. The Voice sang "Come Fly with Me." The Voice sang "Strangers in the Night." The Voice sang "I did it My Way." And our preacher notes in amazement that from 1946 to the present an estimated ten million children have been conceived as The Voice filled American bedrooms.

There it is. She has it. To call Jesus The Word is like calling Frank Sinatra The Voice. The Word. The Voice. But then she starts to wonder. Is this comparison illuminating? Or trivializing? As a preacher, are you helping listeners grasp an elusive title for our Lord by connecting it with a familiar one for Frank Sinatra? Or are you demeaning our Lord by comparing him to a singer who did it his way often enough to end up permanently on the border between fame and notoriety?

Given their setting, preachers need good judgment about the use of illustrations from their reading.

Small and Steady Will Do It

Meanwhile, many of the authors of classic works of literature are still out there for the preacher who wants to bring their treasures forward into sermons. Homer's stories are as stirring today as they ever were, and even children can feel their power. The Sirens still sing. So do Dickens and Hugo and Jane Austen, as we know from the commercial viability of movies and plays based on their stories.

I do not think it realistic to recommend to busy preachers that they read a great novel a week or even a great novel a month. Eugene Peterson appears to have absorbed a large number of great books while pastoring Christ Our King Presbyterian Church in Maryland, but, then, Eugene Peterson is an unusual Christian man.[22] The average minister probably won't read six classic novels in a year, but how about one? Read one great novel a year — or in the case of Tolstoy and Dostoevsky, perhaps a novel's equivalent in four or five short stories. One great novel, read slowly enough, with some pondering and with thoughtful notes taken and stored (including notes on possible connections with sermons) will generate treasure. Five years of this and our preacher will have significant riches from five of the best works anybody ever thought to write.

Just one novel a year? And one biography? And one-fifth of a book of poetry by one poet? And a weekly visit to the website Arts & Letters Daily to find out what the best journalists have been saying?

Not a bad plan, I think.

A Disclaimer

Before I conclude this chapter I want to add a disclaimer that I hope is not too obvious to mention. I mean this: good sermon design and good illustrations and top-quality sermon prose and all the rest of the craft of preaching guarantee nothing where faithful and effective preaching of God's Word is concerned. For one thing, excellent craft can be used in the service of preaching baloney, including pernicious baloney. For another, the preacher may set sail of a Sunday morning with a sermon that is honestly

22. The standard anecdote about Peterson's reading is that he would schedule his reading times into the weekly calendar, e.g., Tuesday and Thursday, 1:30 to 3 p.m., Dostoevsky. People calling the office and asking for Peterson during those times would be told, "I'm sorry, he has someone in the office."

built, but nothing much is going to happen unless the Holy Spirit blows the sermon home.

The Spirit blows where it wills and with peculiar results. As every preacher knows, a nicely crafted sermon sometimes falls flat. People listen to it with mild interest, and then they go home. On other Sundays a preacher will walk to the pulpit with a sermon that has been only roughly framed up in her mind. The preacher has been busy all week with funerals and youth retreats, and on Sunday morning she is not ready to preach. Miraculously, her rough sermon arises in its might and gathers people to God.

Strange things happen when a minister preaches. After the service, people thank the preacher for things she had not said or for things she had said but had not understood as well as the listener had. Our words can be "wiser than we are," Ben Belitt once said, and never more so than when the Spirit of God is in the building.[23]

But the unpredictability of the preaching event gives no one license to wing it. Faithful preachers work hard on their sermons, understanding that although a fruitful result may be God's gift, hard work is the preacher's calling.

After all, it is audacious to speak for God.

23. The poet Ben Belitt said this to Kathleen Norris when she was a freshman in college. See Kathleen Norris, *Amazing Grace: A Vocabulary of Faith* (New York: Riverhead, 1998), p. 9.

Chapter 3

Tuning the Preacher's Ear

Every week preachers face the translator's challenge. Like translators, preachers are trying to say in different words the same thing the text says without inadvertently saying a different thing in different words. Even if the preacher challenges the text, he will want to know exactly what he's challenging. Because the Bible is a difficult ancient literature, because there is a hermeneutical gap between its world and ours, because the congregation's local context may affect the acoustics for preaching, the preacher is up against it just to move the text intact from its world to his.

But beyond accuracy, preachers are also called to shape a text for their congregation, to color it for them, to amplify and apply it. This can be most of the sermon. As a preacher, you have to answer a lot of implied questions. What did this text say? What *does* it say? Why does it matter? How is it surprising or alarming or assuring? What parallels or challenges to its message do we experience every day? Where is the good news of Jesus in this text?

All this takes at least minor league linguistic skill. And we understand why. If I'm preaching I have to do all this exploring and interpreting and applying of a text in such a way that the text will likely "take," that it will engage listeners, that it will find traction with them. None of this matters if the Holy Spirit isn't blowing, but if the sermon has been intelligently designed to catch the

Spirit's breath, and if the Spirit actually blows, the result is what we mean when we say that preaching in the church is *eventful.*

In 1989 Walter Brueggemann published his Lyman Beecher Lectures on the eventfulness of preaching in a book titled *Finally Comes the Poet.*[1] Here Brueggemann writes of the power of the preacher's language to break open closed systems, to smash fixed conclusions, and to summon the brave new world of God. According to Brueggemann, the preacher evokes God's big world behind our little one, unshackling us from dreary conventions, and opening the way for possibilities no eye has seen, no ear has heard, no imagination has ever conceived. All week long, we get what is prosaic and depressingly ideological. But on Sunday, finally comes the poet to startle us with the Word of God that shatters before it mends.

This is an inspiring vision, and I am as inspired by it as anyone. But my own goal in this chapter is less heroic. In writing about the preacher's language, Brueggemann sketches a bold metaphysics of preaching. When I write about the preacher's language, and how general reading may improve it, I am less in the land of metaphysics and more in the department of speech communication.

In either location, I believe, the preacher needs to be at least a minor master of language.

Clarity and Her Best Children

Consider the quiet sermons of Barbara Brown Taylor. People love them and for lots of reasons. One is that the sermons are resonant even when the volume level in them is no more than mezzo-piano. The resonance comes from Taylor's practiced attentive-

1. Walter Brueggemann, *Finally Comes the Poet: Daring Speech for Proclamation* (Minneapolis: Fortress, 1989).

ness to God in life's quotidian details and in her sacramental approach to other people. The attentiveness and reverence are in her sermons. So is her inventiveness, which, like God's mercy, seems new every morning.

But one of the first things most readers discover in Taylor's published sermons is that the writing is so skillful. Skillful sermon writing seems to have a lot of the same qualities as skillful non-sermon writing — it's clear enough, for example, that you could definitely report the gist of it to somebody. Clarity includes conceptual coherence, so that, for example, comparisons and contrasts are between items that are actually coordinate. You want to compare pears to pears. (Back in the day, we had a religion reporter in Grand Rapids, Michigan, who would write that speakers at the inter-faith dialogue were "Muslim, Jewish, Catholic, and Christian.")

We want clarity in a sermon, including coherence. During a sermon we listeners do not want to wonder very often as to why one sermon item follows another. Sermons are too short and too important to have to ask ourselves whether what we are now hearing at minute 11 is an explanation of what we just had, or an example of it, or a concession to it, or a new topic altogether. Lostness is a great topic for a sermon, but not a great condition for its audience.

Beyond coherence, clarity includes transparency too. I do not need my minister to preach his doubts; I want him to preach the gospel. But I do want his preaching to reflect that he knows exactly what doubt feels like. I also would like his preaching to reflect that he knows exactly what faith feels like. And on the bedrock claims of the Christian faith, I would like transparency as to what our preacher is proclaiming. Is he telling us that Jesus' resurrection was an event in Jesus' life or not necessarily? I don't think I should have to wonder about that. Disorients me on Easter Sunday.

I also don't want to guess whether my preacher's stories of the amazing things that have happened to him actually have. When my preacher tells us of a dramatic and unrepeatable hunting prank he played on his brothers that went amusingly wrong, I don't want to read later of exactly this same prank in the 1945 Morton Thompson book titled *Joe the Wounded Tennis Player.*

Clarity includes coherence, transparency, and enough precision of thought and language that after church people can take the sermon home. The preacher needs verbal dexterity to achieve these things, and he will need to achieve them if his sermon is going to move us.

I acknowledge that some of the impact of preaching is owed to good things in it that no preacher could learn from reading print. Much of what works on Sunday morning comes from the preacher's pace, pitch, tone, stress patterns, dynamics of volume, bodily expression, and the like. When he is warmed up, our preacher can give us accelerando and rubato, crescendo and decrescendo, legato and staccato and sforzando and everything short of pizzicato in his sermons, but he won't have learned his music from reading John Updike or Anne Tyler. Or, put it more modestly: he will not have learned speech dynamics as *directly* from his reading as from his listening.

Some of the things that make sermons work cannot be gotten directly from written prose and poetry, but some can, and one of them is so basic, so essential, that if the preacher masters it alone, he will be very far down the road.

Diction 101: Rhetorical Pitch

I have diction in mind. Diction includes pronunciation, and for it preachers need to listen to good pronouncers. For instance we would like our preacher to say "terrorist" instead of "ter-rist" and we would like him to say "nuclear" instead of "nucular." In other words, we would like him to listen more to some U.S. Presidents than to others. But the other half of good diction is word choice, and from the masters of it blessings flow. Precision and coherence and transparency depend on it, of course, but so does everything else in a sermon. Saying good preaching depends on good diction is a little like saying good cooking depends on good ingredients.

For brevity's sake, let's focus on just four advantages of good diction, namely, these: first, good diction (that is, good word choice) lets the preacher choose his rhetorical register, whether highbrow or lowbrow. Second, it gives him narrative movement, and, third, verbal economy. Fourth, and especially, good word choice gives our preacher a whole world of power and beauty that comes from the sheer evocativeness of the language he chooses.

Back to Barbara Brown Taylor. I'd like us to note her command of these features of good diction and see what we can learn from them. Here are a few sentences from the title sermon in the Reverend Taylor's volume titled *Home by Another Way:*

[The three wise men] were all glad for a reason to get out of town — because that was clearly where the star was calling them, out — away from everything they knew how to manage and survive, out from under the reputations they had built for themselves, the high expectations, the disappointing returns. And so they set out, one by one, each believing that he was the only one with a star in his eye until they all ran into one another on the road to Jerusalem. . . .[2]

2. Barbara Brown Taylor, *Home by Another Way* (Cambridge, MA: Cowley, 1999), pp. 28-29.

The wise men, says Taylor, were "glad for a reason to get out of town." Each thought he was "the only one with a star in his eye." All were called "out from under the reputations they had built for themselves." "They all ran into one another on the road to Jerusalem."

I do not want to argue about whether it is a good idea for a preacher to invent a back story for the wise men, and especially not argue when inventions of this kind do not compete with the text and do interest us in its characters.

The wise men, says Taylor, are "glad for a reason to get out of town." The phrase sits right in the middle of the formality/informality scale so that in many contexts it will sound neither stuffy on the high side nor slangy on the low. Imagine possible alternatives. What if Taylor's wise men were "gratified at the life opportunity to venture forth from their hamlet" or what if they "just got so hyper to be so outta there." No, says Taylor, they are "glad for a reason to get out of town."

The register here is neither tuxedo formal nor tank top casual. We might call it "upscale colloquial" or "business casual," and add that it will engage a great many listeners, which is why Taylor wanted to use it. Her good choice makes the sermon formal enough to be serious and casual enough to be comfortable to wear.

To gain command of their pitch on the formality/informality scale, preachers can learn a lot from reading Robert Jacks's classic technique book *Just Say the Word*.[3] Jacks tells us how to write for the ear, not the eye. He wants preachers to prepare sermons that speak naturally, using stories, dialogue, and sentence fragments just as a person would in good conversation. Recommending a register something like upscale colloquial, Jacks cau-

3. G. Robert Jacks, *Just Say the Word: Writing for the Ear* (Grand Rapids: Eerdmans, 1996).

tions preachers against high school mall-speak ("I'm, like, 'Wassup?' and he goes, 'Hey!' and I'm like 'You chillaxin?'") and also against an essay-like formality expressed not only by means of the usual adverb suspects ("whence" "thence," "wherefore") but also by the use of so innocent a coordinating conjunction as "for." According to Jacks, we might not notice the awkward formality of this conjunction in a preached sentence till we stop to think about it. Our preacher says "Let us trust God, for we know God's love is true." We do not stop to think that in ordinary speech none of us talks like that. None of us says "Let's go to Alfredo's tonight, dear, for we know their rigatoni is terrific."[4]

I am not suggesting that if the preacher has upscale colloquial in his repertoire he has the only register he needs. Everything depends on context and audience. A campfire talk to middle school kids will be more casual. A speech at the hundredth anniversary of the congregation might be more formal. In any case, the preacher's reading can give him some rhetorical options. He will want to read storytellers for dialogue, maybe including Jonathan Franzen for contemporary college-educated patterns, and also some of the action and detection types like Elmore Leonard and Lee Child for a little more spit and vinegar.

Published storytellers are good at their job in part because they know how people talk, and the preacher who wants an ear for colloquial dialogue can learn a lot from them. Contractions, sentence fragments, slang, dialect — or grace and elegance — it's all there. If our preacher has a sharp enough ear for dialogue without reading storytellers, God bless him and his natural gifts. But many of the rest of us can use some outside help.

Speaking of which, Elmore Leonard once published ten rules for effective writing, including rule 4: "Never use an adverb to mod-

4. Jacks, *Just Say the Word,* p. 38.

ify the verb 'said.' "[5] *Never use an adverb to modify the verb "said"* Elmore Leonard said gravely. The preacher will take heed. Else on Sunday morning we get, "You hypocrites," Jesus said sternly. "You brood of vipers," he said accusingly. Adverbs give us what is already obvious, or, on the other side of the street, what is not obvious at all and ought to stay that way. Do we really want our preacher's adverbs to tell us how Pilate asked his famous question? "What is truth?" Pilate said amiably. "What is truth?" Pilate said enthusiastically. Or ironically. Or sarcastically. Or who knows, except that he said it interrogatively, and now we're back to what's obvious.

Elmore's tenth commandment for writers, including our preacher, is this: "Leave out the part that people will skip."

Preachers can tune their ear for colloquial language by listening to people talk and by reading dialogue in good writers. That's *colloquial* language. On the other end of the formality scale, the preacher wants enough exposure to classic rhetorical forms to have them in his repertoire and ready to go when called for. Take this example from a eulogy by Ted Kennedy for his slain brother Robert:

> My brother need not be idealized, or enlarged in death beyond what he was in life; to be remembered simply as a good and decent man, who saw wrong and tried to right it, saw suffering and tried to heal it, saw war and tried to stop it.[6]

This form is called symploce, and it is very old and delightful. In symploce you hold the beginnings and ends of the units constant and change the middle in each repetition:

5. "Writers on Writing; Easy on the Adverbs, Exclamation Points and Especially Hooptedoodle," *The New York Times,* July 16, 2001.
6. Full text at www.americanrhetoric.com/speeches/ekennedytributetorfk .html.

[He] **saw** wrong and tried to right **it, saw** suffering and tried to heal **it, saw** war and tried to stop **it.**

Saw-saw-saw, it-it-it. The rhetorical pitch is heightened here by the grammatical structure, not the vocabulary. Most of the words are one syllable, and none is fancy. Yet, as my colleague James Vanden Bosch has pointed out to me, the rhetorical structure all by itself signals the command of the speaker and the weight of the occasion. The preacher who wants similar command can read great speeches, of course, but also great essayists like George Orwell or even editorialists who may reach for a classical form when the occasion is weighty enough.

For those of us who preach, I suppose we generally use the classical rhetorical devices sparingly. If I litter my sermon with them I can start to sound stagy. But for the peak moments, they may be powerful. And, of course, willingly or not, I'm going to have them in my sermons if I quote the psalms. The psalms are full of anaphora, for instance, in which the beginning of successive lines is held constant:

Sing to the Lord . . . Sing to the Lord . . . Sing to the Lord . . .

Ascribe to the Lord . . . Ascribe to the Lord . . . Ascribe to the Lord . . .

How long, O Lord? How long . . .? How long . . .?

Come to think of it, none of this sounds very stagy at all.

Diction 102: Narrative Movement

Back to Barbara Brown Taylor. Her diction lets her pitch her sermon on an upscale colloquial note. Let me now add a second advantage: her good diction also makes her sermon *move*. In the present example, all the movement is centrifugal. The wise men are glad to *get* out, to be *called* out, to *get out from under*, to *set* out, to meet on a road that *leads* out. The wise men are moving out in these sentences, and we listeners move with them.

Preachers who want a similar command of narrative movement can get the feel of it from any of a thousand lively storytellers. Steinbeck's Okies moving off their farms and out onto Route 66. Tim O'Brien's Vietnam grunt soldiers trucking "the things they carried" across the meadows and paddies. Here's William Saroyan's 10-year-old self, a newspaper boy:

> He used to go through the city like an alley cat, prowling all over the place, into saloons, upstairs into whore houses, into gambling joints . . . seeing and smelling, talking, shouting about the big news, inhaling and exhaling, blood moving to the rhythm of the sea, coming and going . . . the boy in the city, walking through it like an alley cat.[7]

As a preacher, I want to read plenty of writers whose characters move. They give me the sense of how to write character movement into my sermons. And, of course, physical motion is just one dimension of narrative movement. Emotions, actions, character development, external circumstances — all of it moves

---

7. William Saroyan, "Resurrection of a Life," in *The Best American Short Stories of the Century*, ed. John Updike, expanded ed. (Boston: Houghton Mifflin, 1999), pp. 159-60.

in lively narrative. Characters push each other's buttons, and respond to getting their buttons pushed, and then push other characters' buttons in turn, and all the while respond to external circumstances that move them along. This is the "circuitry" within narrative.[8]

The deft storyteller will make you want to keep up with the movement and, more, will excite your curiosity about what to expect in the story. William Maxwell, long-term fiction editor at the *New Yorker,* wrote gentle, luminous stories, including some tiny ones he called "improvisations." He tells us that he wrote them to please his wife:

> When we were first married, after we had gone to bed I would tell her a story in the dark. They came from I have no idea where. Sometimes I fell asleep in the middle of a story and she would shake me and say, "What happened next?" and I would struggle up through layers of oblivion and tell her.[9]

Diction 103: Economy

Back to Taylor, who speaks at just the level of formality she wants, and who makes her characters move. She also exhibits a nice verbal economy.

Good preachers don't use more words than they have to. It's not just that padding is an unstylish excess, an example of poor homiletic craftsmanship. It's also that empty calories in a sermon don't feed the flock. There is nothing in them.

8. Thomas McCormack, *The Fiction Editor, the Novel, and the Novelist,* 2nd ed. (Philadelphia: Paul Dry, 2006), p. 30.
9. William Maxwell, *All the Days and Nights: The Collected Stories* (New York: Vintage, 1995), p. x.

I suppose we all have our own ideas of the kinds of verbiage we can do without on a Sunday morning. Meaningless repetition, of course: "Jesus saw that the man was blind. He was blind. He could not see. His eyes were dark. Things were hard for him to spot. All because he was blind."

In his book *Pitfalls in Preaching* Richard Eslinger suggests that preachers should avoid word strings, including doublets such as peace and justice. Each state of affairs is excellent by itself, and the preacher needn't pair them up. I might say the same about honesty and integrity, which significantly overlap. Integrity includes honesty, so we don't need to hear, as we always do, that so-and-so was a woman of honesty and integrity. In any case, congregations do not hear items in word strings distinctly. The preacher says "peace and justice" or "honesty and integrity" or "kindness and compassion and love" and the items blur into each other.[10]

The old rule for tight writing is that every slaughtered syllable is a good deed, and it is true, and it can also be carried too far. If I slay syllables left and right till nothing is left of the sermon but distillate, listeners are going to want to add water.

Verbal economy is an excellent idea, but I don't want to get carried away with it. If I pack my sermon too tight it becomes unlistenable. Eliminate clarifying subordinating conjunctions and I lose my conceptual map. Compact too many observations into aphorisms and I will sound cloying. Cut most verbs, and I'll sound like the elder President Bush. "Natural disasters? Out of bounds. San Francisco earthquake? Not my fault. San Andreas fault."[11]

10. Richard Eslinger, *Pitfalls in Preaching* (Grand Rapids: Eerdmans, 1996), p. 12.

11. A self-parody by President George H. W. Bush, spoken at the 105th annual Gridiron Club Dinner, Washington, DC.

But still, and nevertheless, and however, and all allowances made, the disciplined preacher will cut verbiage. Ernest Campbell, who was senior minister of the Riverside Church in Manhattan in the 1970s, once said in my earshot that the idea with sermons is to write them big — say, half again as big as you need, and then trim them down. What you want, generally speaking, is to "prune luxuriance instead of fanning scarcity."

Good preachers do not say too much. Restraint is part of their craft so they practice it. They don't want to feed people empty calories. But they also understand that *power* can lie not only in what is said but also in what is withheld. Sermons need to be clear, but they don't need to be obvious. So preachers use a bit of indirection, drop a hint, play seven tones of the scale and let us listeners finish in our head. Now we listeners get active. We start to wonder. We begin to imagine.

Barbara Brown Taylor's wise men are glad to get out of town. Why is that? We get hints from her, but not much more, and that is part of the magic.

Good writers don't explain everything. If his character has a guilty conscience, a novelist needn't state that his character has a guilty conscience and then describe his character's guilty feelings. He might do that, but then, again, he might let us *discover* his character's guilty state of mind, as Khaled Hosseini does in *The Kite Runner*.[12] His protagonist Amir has betrayed his best friend, and gradually the symptoms of his guilt start to show up. He can't sleep. He can't eat. He avoids his friend, or he mistreats him, or he projects his own guilt onto him.[13]

Kosseini is following the old rule, which is "Show, don't tell."

---

12. Khaled Hosseini, *The Kite Runner* (New York: Riverhead, 2003), pp. 86-93, 105-7.
13. " 'Shut up!' he explained."

The verbally thrifty preacher can learn how to do it from reading Kosseini or a hundred other writers.

Everything depends on good diction. Clarity depends on it, including coherence and transparency and precision. Rhetorical register depends on it and narrative movement and verbal economy. By reading fine writers, noting their command of language, absorbing it, making it their own in a way relevant to their own preaching context, preachers may strengthen their grasp of language, their first tool.

Fine writers can teach the preacher a little about euphony, too, which is another virtue of Barbara Brown Taylor's writing. The preacher reading the masters may pick up a feel for sentence rhythm and also such rhetorical devices as consonance. He can learn to change up his sentence lengths and sentence functions, such as declaring, questioning, commanding, exclaiming. He can learn Ring Lardner's most famous sentence: "'Shut up,' he explained."

Many of these virtues may be found in a particular literature that preachers might not think of immediately as a sterling resource for their preaching. But I want to lift it up as one of the very most valuable — and, by the way, also one of the most delightful.

I have in mind good children's literature, and I don't think any preacher should be without it. After all, recall from the Preface that books written for children are never written only for them. As Tolkien saw, such books are written for the *childlike*. They move us into a world where we can see with young eyes what children fear, whom they trust, why they hope with such heartbreaking conviction. We see that adults do not always respect children's intelligence and sense of fair play, and that children can be indignant at such folly. The preacher making friends with children's literature will remember that children were important to Jesus, prime exemplars of those who receive the loving power of God and simply live off it.[14]

But for my purpose in this chapter, I want to observe that good children's literature also has a quality of prose that the preacher may want. For clarity and economy, nothing beats simplicity, and here children's books can be a boon to preachers. Perhaps we could call the quality of prose we're looking for "deep simplicity," or, following Vatican II in its recommendation of the type of vernacular wanted for celebrating the eucharist, "noble simplicity."[15] We have all read or heard noble simplicity in great children's literature: "They say Aslan is on the move — perhaps has already landed . . .":

"If there's anyone who can appear before Aslan without their knees knocking, they're either braver than most or else just silly."

"Then he isn't safe?" said Lucy.

"Safe?" said Mr. Beaver. . . . "Course he isn't safe. But he's good. He's the king, I tell you."[16]

Preachers whose language finds noble simplicity will see that their delighted audience includes not just 10-year-olds but also their parents and grandparents, because in the heart of every adult there still lives a child who can be moved by a story.

Let me add that clarity and economy are not merely rhetori-

14. Gary D. Schmidt, author of such prizewinning novels as *Lizzie Bright and the Buckminster Boy* (2004) and *The Wednesday Wars* (2007), makes such observations in his regular visits to "Imaginative Reading for Creative Preaching," a summer seminar at Calvin College, underwritten by the Center for Excellence in Preaching of Calvin Theological Seminary.

15. I owe this point to John Witvliet.

16. C. S. Lewis, *The Lion, the Witch and the Wardrobe* (New York: Scholastic, 1978), pp. 67, 80.

cal virtues. They are character virtues too. Without becoming obvious or clunky, the clear preacher obeys one of the great commandments: don't drive your listeners nuts. If they cannot figure out what you are trying to say, they will get cranky. The concise preacher obeys a second great commandment too: don't waste your listeners' time. Don't make them wait while you unfold layers of padding. The preacher with noble simplicity obeys a third commandment as well: delight your listeners whenever you can. When they are delighted, they want to praise Jesus.

Let's add that all three of these commandments — don't frustrate, don't waste people's time, do delight them once in a while — follow from God's command in Leviticus and Jesus' repetition of it in the gospel, namely, "Love your neighbor as yourself."

Diction 104: Evocativeness

I have been praising good diction for giving the preacher a command of pitch and movement and verbal economy including simplicity. And then, of course, good diction gives a preacher the power to evoke, to suggest, and therefore to move our hearts.

The wise men, says Barbara Brown Taylor, were "glad for a reason to get out of town." Each thought he was "the only one with a star in his eye." All were called "out from under the reputations they had built for themselves." And "they all ran into one another on the road to Jerusalem."

This is evocative writing. It makes you ponder, makes you wonder, makes you yearn a little. If reading good writing cannot improve the evocative power of my sermon prose, I'm probably a lost cause. The good writers are masters of turning a phrase, turning a clause, turning a sentence — all because again and again they choose one word instead of another:

"He was so careful of the truth that he used it sparingly"
(Ross Macdonald).

"I grew up in the shadow of a big bookcase" (Baudelaire).

"He was tubby and coarse-featured, with bulbous eyes and
bristly hair mown short by a barber with a heavy hand"
(Michael Thomas).

Here's Steinbeck in *East of Eden:* "I remember that the Gabilan Mountains to the east of the valley were light gray mountains full of sun and loneliness and a kind of invitation, so that you wanted to climb into their warm foothills almost as you want to climb into the lap of a beloved mother."[17]

In thinking about the evocative power of fine diction consider the essayist Edward Hoagland, who is a naturalist often compared to Thoreau. Hoagland is the sort of keen observer who appears never to have forgotten anything striking he has seen outdoors, which is a lot to remember when you have been outdoors all your life. Hoagland spots wonders outdoors and so helps preachers refresh their love of God's good creation and their inclination to celebrate it.

But Hoagland also possesses a sovereign command of the English language, and so the preacher can learn some diction from him. Early in his autobiographical essay titled "Small Silences"[18] he tells of moving to a Connecticut farm at age 8. The farm had "a little brook running" through it, which made wonderful sounds, "thocking and ticking, bubbling and trickling." It rippled, but it also mirrored, and it would tug on a boy's fingers or feet when he dipped them in.

For their egg supply, Hoagland's parents kept a dozen brown

17. John Steinbeck, *East of Eden* (New York: Viking, 1952), p. 3.
18. In *Sex and the River Styx* (White River Junction, VT: Chelsea Green, 2011).

hens, and then bought a New Hampshire Red rooster "to trumpet their accomplishments." The red rooster didn't go off in the morning mechanically, like an alarm clock. No, the rooster knew that in the night eight hens had laid eight eggs and that at dawn it was time to celebrate at least eight times. So the rooster would raise his beak and "trumpet the accomplishments" of the hens.

Let's say our preacher notes the trumpeting, and some months later is preaching from one of the visions of shalom in Isaiah. Might there be a place in his sermon to extend the prophet's dream of perfect peace, harmony, and delight in creation by suggesting that in this blessed state the red roosters graciously crow over the accomplishments of the hens?

Of course, but the trumpeting rooster is valuable to the preacher even if never mentioned explicitly in a sermon. The reason is that good diction in writers inspires preachers to imagine possibilities of their own. The preacher's ear is tuned by absorbing excellent language, even if unconsciously. He's like an articulate child from a family of articulate speakers, except that the preacher's professional family includes Marilynne Robinson and Edward Hoagland and Katherine Paterson and John Steinbeck and so many others.

Alas, preachers who understand the evocative power of terrific diction can get distracted by it and start composing sermons not so much to preach the gospel of Jesus Christ as to enchant us with their words. A preacher reads good writers and feels their power to evoke, and the power moves him. In fact, it moves him to want to do the same thing for his congregation. So maybe he composes sermons intended to be atmospheric. The preacher hopes to cast a spell, perhaps, and so chooses words for the likelihood that they will send everybody home with a soul full of yearning.

Along the way, our preacher figures out who the great homiletic spell casters are and so becomes a bad imitator of Frederick Buechner. Buechner has published a number of famously evocative sermons with evocative titles, such as "The Hungering Dark" and "The Magnificent Defeat." "The Magnificent Defeat" is a sermon from Genesis 32 about Jacob at the ford of the Jabbok River. Jacob is on the threshold of a meeting with his brother Esau after years of estrangement. Because he caused the estrangement, Jacob isn't sleeping well the night before the reunion, and especially because he has to wrestle all night with a mysterious stranger.

When dawn breaks enough for Jacob to see the stranger's face, what he sees, says Buechner, is "something more terrible than the face of death — the face of love. It is vast and strong, half ruined with suffering and fierce with joy, the face a man flees down all the darkness of his days until at last he cries out, 'I will not let you go, unless you bless me.' "[19]

This is virtuoso writing, and our preacher loves it. Figuring that nobody writes like this without having carried on an earnest conversation with poets and storytellers, our preacher starts the conversation in hope of casting a few Buechner spells of his own. He tries to imitate Buechner's virtuosity and without much luck. Buechner is almost inimitable, and bad Buechner imitations are very bad sermons, full of mystifying wisps and vapors. You try to capture some of the vapors to take home to your spouse who was sick that morning, and as you drive home the Sunday sermon evaporates in your car.

Preachers who try too hard to cast a spell with the power of their diction will probably not often succeed. Life so often releases its gifts only if we do not try hard for them. I am thinking of such things as making friends or getting to sleep or becoming an

19. "The Magnificent Defeat," in *A Chorus of Witnesses*, ed. Thomas G. Long and Cornelius Plantinga Jr. (Grand Rapids: Eerdmans, 1994), p. 10.

original thinker or making a good impression in a job interview or becoming happy in life. Try too hard at any of these things and we defeat ourselves. Faith in God is itself much more gift and discovery than deliberate achievement.

My point is that all the powers of language the preacher picks up from listening and reading are means, not ends, and that the preacher is called not just to linguistic craft but to faithful proclamation of reconciling grace in Jesus Christ. The power and glory may happen, but not so much because the preacher wanted them to. They happen because of the mighty and mysterious work of the Holy Spirit.

And so it was on August 28, 1963, a day forever to be remembered in American history because the power of a preacher's evocative diction and the movement of the Holy Spirit combined within the greatest sermon ever delivered to the nation. In this sermon Martin Luther King Jr. preached justice from the prophets and he did it without apology and without disguise. He was a preacher to the nation that day, who sounded his sermon refrain and then sounded it again. "I have a dream," he said. "I have a dream today."

Longing was in that word, and frank recognition of sad reality. Hope was in that word, and imagination. A different word chosen for the refrain and we would not now be remembering the speech. "I have a dream. I have a dream today."

Jean Bethke Elshtain has speculated that American civil rights history might have gone quite differently if King had stood before the Lincoln Memorial on August 28, 1963 and cried out to the nation "I have a personal preference. I have a personal preference today."[20]

Good diction can give the preacher clarity and all her chil-

20. "Everything for Sale," *Books & Culture*, May/June 1998, p. 9.

dren. Good diction can give him an apt rhetorical register, and lively narrative movement, and conciseness, and a whole wide world opened by the deliberate choice of this word instead of that one.

"I have a dream. I have a dream today."

Chapter 4

Whatever You Get, Get Wisdom

The weekly assignment to preach the gospel of grace in Jesus Christ is daunting. Maybe half a million English-language preachers got up to preach this past Sunday, and I would like us to appreciate the hill they climbed.

Where else in North American life today do we find a speaking assignment that is comparable? Where else is a man or a woman called forward once a week to address a mixed audience on things of final magnificence?

For starters, the address has to *change* all the time. A politician can take a stump speech to LA or Miami and customize one minute of it for the local context. Else it's the same speech. Our regular church minister has just the reverse situation: it's the audience that stays the same week after week and the address that needs to change.

Mixed Audience

That's one daunting thing. Here is another: because it is mixed, the preacher's audience calls for great tact on her part. Her listeners may be young or old, educated or not, emotionally fragile or secure, prosperous or scraping by. They may be racially and ethnically mixed. Even if not, the congregants may be Democrats or Republicans, culturally progressive or conservative. So if in a sermon our preacher refers to, say, Donald Trump and does so in a breezy tone, a quarter of the congregation thinks she has condescended to an important national leader. But if she refers to Mr. Trump in a respectful tone, a different quarter thinks she has dignified a buffoon.

In some settings, the congregational mix may be morally and religiously significant, too. Some of the congregants believe that an agonized decision to end a pregnancy may sometimes be justified while others believe that abortion is always a form of homicide. Both groups hold their position tenaciously and each may think the other is morally tainted.

Some in the congregation are evangelistically minded. They know that the gospel is for the lost and they think it's every church member's duty to reach them with it. But others think of evangelism as embarrassing or even as a sort of imperialism. Some in the congregation are inclined to emotional, even bodily, expressions of their faith such as swaying and arm-raising and crying Hallelujah in worship while others find their faith better expressed in the Book of Order of the Presbyterian Church in the United States of America. Some love ardor and some love order.

All of these Christians — young, old, rich, poor, progressive, conservative, pro-choice, pro-life, plus everybody with heartfelt positions on LGBT issues — are people our preacher speaks to about life and death, about sex and sexual identity, about witnessing for Jesus, about an urgent city-wide referendum on housing that is really about immigration. And then, every so often, the preacher has to talk to people about their money.

The preacher's task is formidable. She may touch people's hearts with a serious program of preaching, but she is at least as likely to touch their nerves, and she will know only some of the time *which* nerves a sermon will touch.

Some in the audience are teens, who are human just like the rest of us, only more so. When my brother Leon was a teen he wrote to Ann Landers as follows: "Dear Ann Landers. I am sixteen. Can you help me?" Teens are some of the most interesting people on the planet, and if the preacher is naïve about her teenage audience, trouble awaits.

Think of a naïve and lovable preacher who had barely noticed, and had never thought about, a remarkable fact of contemporary retailing. In the shopping mall our loveable preacher observes that jeans for sale to teens are sold as new when they are already ragged in the knees and thighs. That is remarkable to the preacher and even more because the ragged jeans are just as expensive as the others. To the preacher this is a juicy irony that belongs in a sermon.

The problem is that to the 15-year-olds in the congregation there is nothing funny or ironic about expensive ragged jeans, and the preacher who mocks the jeans simply loses a part of the congregation and maybe for quite a while.

The preacher constantly has to judge how she will be heard. Maybe her audience is young and suburban, or maybe it is elderly and rural, or maybe it is mostly upscale professionals in Manhattan. Think of how a biblical word like "hope" might sound in these very different settings with their very different acoustics.

Maybe our preacher's people are half immigrants and only some of them have papers and the ones who do not are sitting in church afraid, because they are afraid wherever they sit. Most of her listeners on Sunday morning may be native English speakers, but maybe not all of them.

Now the preacher has a diction question. To engage the brothers and sisters with less English would seem to require different pulpit diction than to engage native speakers. What's the preacher to do? Speak very plainly and slowly? Or is that patronizing? Avoid word play, or explain it, or limit it to one little burst a week, or what?

After a stroke in 1999, William Sloan Coffin — the activist chaplain at Yale University in the 1960s and 1970s and later senior minister of Riverside Church in New York — was back on Yale's campus in 2003 to address one of the class reunions. A man I know was there. As Coffin began to talk, some of the listeners were shocked. His stroke had significantly impaired his speech and he was slurring enough to be hard to understand.

Coffin grasped their reaction and quipped about Mark Twain. Twain, he said, had once assured an audience that Wagner's music was actually "better than it sounded." Coffin hoped people would conclude the same about his address to them that day.

The quip, with its easy sophistication, worked fine on Yale's campus, but what if the audience had been less educated or speakers of English as a second language or lovers of hip-hop who had never heard of Richard Wagner?

The call to preach is formidable: our preacher has multiple decisions to make based simply on knowledge of her audience. Is this a congregation dominated by four powerful families, two of which employ a third of the congregation? How did this play out in the congregation the last time the company had to lay people off? And what is the residue when the sermon is about unity in the church?

The preacher constantly has to read her context and adapt to it. Was this congregation deceived by its last pastor, who was leading a double life? Are some members now tender on the topic of ministerial hypocrisy? What does this say to the preacher about her choice of sermon texts? Does it put Matthew 23, with its sevenfold indictment of religious hypocrites, *on* the preaching schedule or *off* it?

In what frame of mind do people come to church of a Sunday morning? There may be a broken heart in every pew, as my colleague Hulitt Gloer reminds me, but there is also an ebullient heart in every pew, so that the preacher's text and mood won't fit everybody, and our preacher knows this while preparing the sermon.

What about preaching on marital fidelity when the ghosts of so many old divorces hover over the pews? How about ignoring marriage altogether, given that half the congregation under forty thinks the institution is quaint? How about lifting up this classical institution and calling attention to its advantages?

Considerations of these kinds require a lot of wisdom from the preacher, and so far I have been facing only the fact that the preacher stands before a mixed audience. Other variables cluster in the neighborhood too.

What difference, for instance, does the preacher's own personal and pastoral identity make to the authenticity of her preaching? That she is learned, for instance. That she is married and that her husband is spotty in church attendance. That she is a skilled provocateur. That she is female. That she ministers in a blue state and also loves NASCAR? (Her disconnect here is that people in blue states find auto races hard to fathom: Why would anybody pay for the privilege of sitting for hours to watch TRAFFIC?)

The preacher needs good judgment all the time. How often can she plausibly speak of economic injustice? What's the line between prophetic witness and scolding? Is there a place for — let's call it rebuke, not scolding — rebuke in a sermon? In the New Testament, Christians rebuke each other quite often and counsel each other about how to do it.

With North American Christians today, not so much. Rebuke sounds judgmental. It's not very tolerant. But what if somebody makes a clearly racist remark at a congregational meeting? Tolerance under the circumstances would seem cowardly. But is there a way to rebuke with minimum necessary force, and with escalating pressure, as necessary? Does our preacher know how to do this? Has she been to a rebuke workshop?

Can she address materialism if she drives a convertible? A Miata convertible OK, but not a small Mercedes? Not even a small old Mercedes? Not even a small old Mercedes which was a gift from her Uncle Wally?

What happens when a personally dominant preacher speaks on meekness? Or when a quiet and buttoned-up preacher celebrates boldness for the Lord and for the gospel?

The central thing I want us to face in this chapter is that the preacher has a daunting task and to meet it she is going to need a great deal of wisdom.

A Sketch of Wisdom

Following some biblical themes, let's say that wisdom is a reality-based phenomenon: the wise are people who know human life and how to live it faithfully. They have an unusually rich understanding of God and of God's world and of how to fit into it. They respect the transcendence of God and don't try to domesticate God. They treasure the immanence of God and don't try to abstract God from ordinary life. They trust Jesus Christ, the wisdom of God, who upsets much of what passes for wisdom in the world.

The wise know how human life goes — its times and seasons, its patterns and dynamics, its laws and rhythms. They know that whatever you sow you will reap, which is not only a biblical proverb, but also a cry from the depths in much of the world's great literature.

The wise are discerning. A discerning person picks up on

things. She notices the difference between pleasure and joy, for example, and between sentimentality and compassion. She understands that facts are stubborn things, and doesn't try to finesse them to suit her wishes. She discerns the differences between things but also the connections between them.[1]

She knows creation — what God has put together and what God has kept apart — and can therefore spot the fractures and alloys produced by those who violate creation. She knows a number of the ironies of life, including that it is possible to be "a good person in the worst sense of the word," namely, one who offers help in ways that make people wish he hadn't bothered.

She knows ironies and oddities of life under the sun — that mercy sometimes coexists with mendacity, for example, and kindness with lust. She is good at estimating causes and effects, including human motives and consequences. She can spot patterns in behavior and take them more seriously than isolated acts. She understands that people full of shadows may also be full of a light that causes them. In such and other respects, Lewis Smedes remarks, "a discerning person has the makings of a connoisseur."[2]

Of course our preacher needs much more than discernment. To thrive in her ministry she needs faith and learning and courage to lead. She needs a prayer life and a social life. She needs an intelligent sense of her pastoral identity, and some of the humor and self-irony that keep it healthy. She needs the grace of God just to get up in the morning and face her daunting task.

But whatever she gets to help her face it, she will need to get wisdom. The Book of Proverbs says "Get wisdom, and whatever

---

1. Lewis B. Smedes, *A Pretty Good Person* (San Francisco: Harper & Row, 1990), p. 123.
2. Smedes, *A Pretty Good Person*, p. 128.

else you get, get insight" (4:7). That is, get attentiveness, get discernment, get good judgment. Try to get some emotional intelligence too, such as empathy, because wisdom is never cold. It's always emotionally engaged.

Maybe the wise preacher is simply obedient to Jesus, who said that that we should be as wise as serpents and as innocent as doves (Matt. 10:16). Maybe our preacher will become the sort of person on whom nothing is lost.

Even the skills of her craft count as part of her wisdom, I think, because wisdom is always practical. The wise know life but also how to go at it. They have some skills. They have a knack.

And so the wise preacher, too, will have a knack for her calling. She will read her mixed audience and adapt her preaching accordingly. She will manage the impact on the congregation of her own personal and pastoral identity. She will figure out how to speak to a congregation on blood-warming topics — or, at least, partly figure it out. She'll illustrate a sermon in ways that enlighten and do not distract. She'll develop the kind of sermon diction that fully engages her congregation and sometimes moves their hearts.

Her wide reading is extremely apt to help her manage all this with a healthy degree of wisdom. We have already seen this with respect to illustrations and diction. But it's true with respect to the rest of the preacher's calling as well. Read a context and adapt your address to it? Biographies are full of people who were masters of this — biographies of FDR, for instance, who sold the lend-lease program to a skeptical American public at the start of World War II. Figure out the impact of your own personality and professional identity on your listeners? Storytellers are full of examples of people who are adept at this — every story in the genre of disguised royalty, for instance, such as Mark Twain's story *The Prince and the Pauper.* Figure out how to talk to your audience on blood-warming topics? Journalists do this every day. Call it spin, if you like, or call it diplomacy. In either case, preachers have much to learn from journalists about tact for tough topics.

Becoming a Sage on Everything under the Sun

I recommend a reading program for preachers for lots of reasons, but chiefly because it will tend to make the preacher wise. It will give her substance. This is especially so, I believe, with respect to one huge and obvious part of our preacher's calling. Week by week the preacher has to have something intelligent to say on an intimidating list of topics raised by biblical texts. To do so she will need to become a minor expert on a good number of them.

What topics? Everything under the sun that's in the Bible: God, sin, grace, the beauty of creation, life, death, justice, the Kingdom of God, faith, hope, love, the death of Jesus, compassion, peace, comfort, the miracle of Easter, pilgrimage, aging, wonder, the ascension of Jesus, terror, alienation, hell, the judgment of God, longing, betrayal, redemption, the joy of heaven. The list of topics on the preacher's agenda intimidates all but the foolish. And I have given only a partial list because the Bible is such a big book.

Now add that the congregation sends its preacher to the Bible not just to dig up its treasures and lay them out on Sunday morning, but also to do so in such a way that, with the Holy Spirit blowing in the room, the minister's words may bring *God's* Word to us.

The preacher has to become a kind of sage, a person who is conversant on biblical topics — and this is so even if she is an expository preacher, because if the Bible touches on a topic the preacher has to follow suit. Maybe she will know quite a lot about biblical topics from her experience of life and her experience of life in the congregation. Undoubtedly she will know a lot about them from the Bible itself. But the Bible doesn't tell us everything about its topics. "Forgive," Jesus says. But exactly what does forgiveness consist in? "Be angry, but do not sin," Ephesians says. But how would that go, given how volatile anger can be? "Love is patient and love is kind," says St. Paul. OK, but that's just the first two seconds of the sermon. What does the preacher have to say for the twenty-three minutes and fifty-eight seconds that follow?

She may need some help. She may need all the harvest of her conversation with storytellers, biographers, poets, and journalists.

After all, general literature abounds in incidents, characters, images, and observations that *illumine* everything under the sun, including most of the topics on which the preacher has to become at least a middleweight sage.

Let me add at once that the preacher in quest of wisdom is realistic about what a program of general reading will yield. She doesn't need her reading to yield one desperately deep insight after another that, once ingested, make the preacher more profound than everybody in the philosophy department. Of course she would like to draw more from her reading than mere commonplaces, but she doesn't expect her soul to shatter and mend every time she sits to read.

Examples of "Middle Wisdom"

Perhaps the preacher is hoping to acquire from her reading what I call "middle wisdom." Let's say that middle wisdom consists of insights into life that are more profound than commonplaces, but less so than great proverbs. A great proverb such as "pride goes before destruction" (Prov. 18:16) arises from a depth of centuries and compacts in itself all the experience of those centuries.

Middle wisdom is more modest. It's middleweight insight. Still, it's definitely worth acquiring: it can save the preacher from some of the dreaded follies of the pulpit. I'm thinking of banality in the pulpit. Presumption too. Vagueness doesn't help anybody, and neither does dogmatism. Vagueness and dogmatism are an especially foolish combination, and ministers aren't the only people plagued with it. In academe, for instance, people will sometimes write something that's utterly elusive, and then insist on it.

William Maxwell once wrote a story titled "The Carpenter," which is a fairy tale with a "turn" in it, a bad one.[3] In this tale, the village carpenter builds honestly. Everything about him is square. He sawed according to the "even rhythm of his heartbeat," and "used his carpenter's rule and stubby pencil as if he were applying a moral principle." Meanwhile, villagers would come into the shop one at a time, close the door, and watch for a while. But then would come the moment when the visitor would say, " 'I know I can trust you because you don't repeat anything . . .'" What followed was always a secret that if it got out would ruin life for some other villager.

The carpenter hadn't asked to collect secrets in this way, and there came a season of his life when he began to resent being used as a repository. So he took revenge on the secrets by betraying one of them. Then he betrayed another. Then, one day, he started a damaging rumor that if it got out would get the village fiddler killed. At the end of the story the carpenter still saws and cuts in his shop, but now his plane jams more than it used to and

---

3. William Maxwell, "The Carpenter," in his *All the Days and Nights: The Collected Stories* (New York: Vintage, 1995), pp. 341-44.

his saw won't follow the pencil line cleanly. Even his tools are no longer honest.

What's the middle wisdom to be derived from the story? I don't know what Maxwell wanted to teach in it. Maybe nothing. Artists are seldom didactic in their fiction, or at least seldom admit to being didactic. So let me say only that I gathered a piece of middle wisdom from this story whether or not Maxwell intended it. In reading the story it occurred to me that secrets are potent things. *We may think we are honoring someone by telling him our secret. But the knowledge of it may fester in him and turn to poison. Maybe only God can absorb deep human secrets without internal damage.*

Maybe our preacher will want this piece of middle wisdom on the day she preaches Psalm 139. "Search me, O God, and know my heart." This is not a general invitation for just anybody to rummage around in our hearts. Somebody else might be destroyed by what they find there. But not God. Never God.

In *Remembering Denny*,[4] Calvin Trillin tells of a Yale classmate from the 1950s. Denny Hansen was handsome, funny, and intelligent. He was a golden boy from California, a record-breaking swimmer, a genial magnet for admirers, a Rhodes Scholar, and president of everything he joined. All through school days, his friends kept making bets and jokes about the day when Denny Hansen would be elected President of the United States. Every time Denny met his friends' parents one of them would predict that Denny would end up on the Supreme Court or become Speaker of the House of Representatives. When Denny graduated from Yale, poised to begin his Rhodes Scholarship at Oxford, *Life* magazine was there, and later published a splashy story about Denny Hansen, the boy who had it all.

4. Trillin, *Remembering Denny* (New York: Warner, 1993).

But across the years after college, classmates and friends gradually lost touch with Denny because he did not answer their letters or return their calls. As they later discovered, Denny's career trajectory had flattened out and he had not wanted to say so. After all, he had not become President, or even Speaker of the House. He had never married. His career was a shameful failure: all he had done was to have authored several respected books and occupied a professorship at the Johns Hopkins School of International Relations. And he was homosexual in a time tougher than ours. One day in his middle age the golden boy from California started his car in a closed garage, lay down in it, and ended his life.

We may think we are praising and encouraging the young by predicting great things for them, but the burden of our expectations may shame and crush them.

The preacher learns much about human character from biographies and memoirs. But fiction, too, is famously revealing of it. Here it's interesting to note that goodness is seemingly harder to portray fictionally than evil. Readers find it comparatively boring: a handout is so much less interesting than a stickup. The seven deadly sins are the primary colors for literary artists, not the seven deadly virtues. Still, the great writers understand and portray goodness in ways that preachers need both professionally and personally. Dickens's good characters are often too good (e.g., Esther in *Bleak House*), but some are mostly convincing and, anyhow, deeply encouraging — Peggoty, for instance, in *David Copperfield* and Joe Gargery in *Great Expectations*.

But the truly great achievements of fictional goodness are characters like Thomas Hardy's Mayor of Casterbridge, or, especially, Victor Hugo's Jean Valjean, whose motives and history make them riven and shadowed figures. The goodness that emerges in these characters is all the more believable for being scarred and rough. Can anyone preach the Bible's Peter or Paul without a broad background understanding of what it is to be a man with a past?

Scripture Still Rules

I'm not suggesting for a moment that my job as a preacher is to bring a literary understanding of life to Scripture and then preach only the part of Scripture that confirms what I had already picked up from Toni Morrison or Cormac McCarthy. Just the opposite: Scripture is our community's book on the big issues, and it often shatters received knowledge and upsets the wisdom of this world.

Jesus Christ, the wisdom of God, was in his crucifixion an example of folly to the Greeks. The program of Jesus in the world, then and now, cuts *against* the grain of conventional wisdom. "I believe in Jesus Christ, God's only Son, our Lord," we say in the Creed, and I commit myself in saying this to the person of Christ, who in his incarnation upset every ancient conviction that God cannot become messy, lowly, fleshy, humiliated, hurt, and dead, and still be God.

Scriptural wisdom upsets a lot of the conventional wisdom of the world. "I believe in Jesus Christ, God's only Son, our Lord." In saying this I commit myself not only to the person of Christ, and to his incarnation, but also to his very counterintuitive program of dying and rising. I need trust to commit to Jesus' program. After all, in his program self-expenditure leads to life, and not just to burnout. I need to trust that in his death Jesus absorbed the world's evil into himself without passing it back, and so cut the loop of vengeance that has cycled down the ages. I need to trust that in his resurrection Jesus opened a door that had always been locked and that he has left it open. And that in his ascended glory

Jesus Christ has given us a new address for heaven so that, if you look it up, heaven's address is wherever Jesus is.

Christ is "the wisdom of God" (1 Cor. 1:24). In one standard theological account of him he is the mediator not only of redemption, but also of creation. To say of him that he is the wisdom of God is a creation metaphor, I believe, before it is a redemption metaphor, and it suggests that the work of Jesus Christ represents the intelligence and expressiveness of the triune God. According to God's intelligence, the way to thrive is to help others to thrive; the way to flourish is to cause others to flourish; the way to fulfill yourself is to spend yourself.

This is a contrarian view in much of the world, ancient and contemporary, and nothing in the preacher's general reading may supplant it. Christ, the wisdom of God, is the standard. The preacher measures her reading *against* the standard. This is a matter of simple but stubborn faith in Jesus Christ, including his program of dying and rising.

So we Christians take on self-denial, and trust that we will not be a fool to do it. We take on humility, and trust that humility is actually a sign of strength and a species of wisdom. We forgive those who have hurt us and trust that we will actually be OK if we give up anger we have a right to.[5]

The preacher's authority in the pulpit does not derive from the lordship of literature. Nothing in my ordination compels me to declare, "Thus saith Philip Roth." But given God's common grace, given that all truth is God's truth, given that the Holy Spirit blows wherever it wants, I may expect my conversations with writers sometimes to give me wisdom consonant with Scripture or, perhaps, even *explanatory* of Scripture.

---

5. I owe this way of putting the matter to Robert C. Roberts.

We Are Not God

Of course there is anti-wisdom out there too. Nihilist writers, casual nihilist writers, materialist writers, highly seductive humanist writers, writers who conflate sex, romance, and love — all kinds of writers are out there. As a preacher I want to know them. I want to learn from them. I want some of them in my sermons. Learning from nihilists and atheists is a bracing thing to do. And it may reveal whether I have actually acquired some of the combined confidence and humility that all of us have seen in good mentors. I want confidence that Christ is the Wisdom of God, with all that such trust entails. I also want humility in the face of intelligent writers who do not trust Christ in the least, but may still have much to teach me.

And maybe humility toward the author of the book in my hand means slowing down when it comes to pegging his or her worldview. I just wrote of nihilist writers, materialist writers, humanist writers. Maybe I should be cautious with such labels.

I once found counsel to this effect in a letter by Stanley Wiersma, who taught English at Calvin College with great distinction during the last century. Be a little slow, he wrote, to think you can spot a great author's worldview. No pontificating, please, on the shaping vision of a work of fiction, and certainly not in order to blow it away in Christian love. How easy and dreary it would be to read in this way. Scott Fitzgerald was wrong in sense A, and the later Mark Twain in sense B, and Jonathan Franzen in sense C, and so on. This would be more like hunting than reading. Seek, kill, carve, serve for lunch.

We always have one simple reason to hesitate about an author's worldview. We are not God. We read authors' novels, not their hearts. Novels are as complicated as people when it comes to naming their dominant vision. Few novels are plain. This is one of the marks of their greatness. Think of how many ways *The Grapes of Wrath* can be read. Is it a social protest novel? Or a biblical epic of pilgrimage to the promised land? Or a story of the triumph of compassion over hardship? Or of solidarity over isolation? Is Steinbeck's vision naturalist? Or pantheist? Or naturalist pantheist? Or mystical naturalist pantheist?

Hard to say, and wonderfully unnecessary, because Steinbeck delivers his wallop no matter what gloves you put on him.

"Whatever you get, get wisdom." Our preacher wants wisdom from the people she reads, and will often get it from writers she cannot finally peg.

By the way, every so often an author will offer up a fine piece of middle wisdom the preacher doesn't need, because she already has it. Suppose our preacher reads Robert Frost's dramatic poem titled "Home Burial."[6] This is a 117-line masterpiece of empathy and insight centering on a man and a woman who have lost a child. She's inconsolable and he's ready to absorb the loss and move on. She grieves by remembering and he by planning. Neither thinks the other has the right recipe for grieving, or the right speed for it, and their quarrel over these things wedges them apart. Frost wrote this poem from sorrowful experience and he wrote it with great depths of understanding.

Frost does not inform our preacher of anything. He confirms what she knows from her pastoral care of grieving parents, and about which she can add whole textures of understanding on top of Frost's. What preachers already know and Frost confirms is that when parents lose a beloved child they often end up losing each other as well.

---

6. Professor Susan Felch masterfully presents "Home Burial" to preachers in the Calvin College Summer Seminar "Imaginative Reading for Creative Preaching," and every time preachers call on their pastoral experience to describe variations on Frost's theme.

Things We Should Not Know

The preacher needs to be a bit of a sage, and wise authors can help. Maybe the preacher will read Roger Shattuck's social criticism. In a book titled *Forbidden Knowledge* Shattuck explores an idea that, since the Enlightenment, has become almost unthinkable, namely, that there might be some things we human beings should not know. "Proverbs in every language tell us that it is possible to know too much for our own good," says Shattuck.[7]

Is this old instinct mere parochialism? Or does it provide us with a healthy warning sign? On January 27, 2012, NBC *Nightly News with Brian Williams* aired a segment about a scientist named Ron Forchier who created what is thought to be the most dangerous virus ever known to man. He took a strain of bird flu, which is typically no threat to humans, and infected ferrets with it, who then infected each other with appalling ease. It turns out that ferret flu is a model of human flu, readily transferable and therefore deadly. Other scientists estimate that if Forchier's virus got out of his lab, it would cause a horrible pandemic, killing perhaps 60 percent of the people it infected.

That the virus might get out of the lab and into the public is only one danger. A bigger one is that the *knowledge* of how to produce the virus might fall into the wrong hands. Two journals, namely *Science* and the second one, *Nature,* had been set to publish Dr. Forchier's research, but a panel that advises the government on health threats asked the journals to suppress critical details, fearing that the full recipe would be irresistible to terrorists.

Why did Dr. Forchier conduct his experiment? Simply, he said, because "I wanted to learn what was possible."

7. Roger Shattuck, *Forbidden Knowledge: From Prometheus to Pornography* (New York: Harcourt Brace, 1996), p. 1.

But are there possibilities we should not explore? Things we should not know? How to create a kind of flu that will kill anybody it infects? What the scene of an airliner crash really looks like? Exactly how long you still have to live? What your friend almost said to you? Precisely what it was like for your parents to have sex?

Roger Shattuck suggests that the writings of the Marquis de Sade provide an excellent example of what is, at minimum, extremely dangerous to know — namely, how to combine cruelty, humiliation, and murder in ways that will excite and sustain lust. Also, how not to ignore the pain you cause in your victims, but revel in it. Shattuck discusses these things and, in the light of them, the astonishing fact that some academics in the last decades have been out to rehabilitate Sade's reputation and save him from the disapproval of censorious types.

In a telling discussion of Book 10 of Augustine's *Confessions,* Shattuck calls attention to Augustine's discussion of *libido sciendi,* the lust for knowledge, and remarks that Augustine thought this lust more perilous than the more ordinary kind, because it can try to rival God's omniscience and thus usurp God's prerogative.

All this, I suggest, is worth the preacher's pondering. What are we to make of the story of the Tree of the Knowledge of Good and Evil of Genesis 2 and the divine prohibition against eating of its fruit? What Godly prerogative is fenced by this prohibition and what human disaster unleashed by flouting it? "You may freely eat of every tree of the garden; but of the tree of the knowledge of good and evil you shall not eat, for in the day that you eat of it you shall die" (Gen. 2:16-17).

When I was a boy I always imagined that these mysterious words were a test of Adam and Eve's obedience, and maybe an arbitrary one. But what if the words are a gracious warning? What if God's prohibition is like that on an electrical power station: Danger! High Voltage! Keep Out!

Maybe the preacher will gather wisdom from Shattuck on forbidden knowledge, or from Garrett Keizer on anger,[8] or from Chiamanda Ngozi Adichie on religious oppression inside one's own home.[9] Maybe our preacher will learn the wiles of self-deception from Daniel Goleman[10] or the torment of being an outsider from Theodore Dreiser.[11] These themes, a tiny sample from hundreds, appear in Scripture and will one day show up in our preacher's sermons. If she has done some reading and thinking on them before she ever sits down to compose her sermon she will already be a good way into her sermon.

Occasionally a work of fiction appears that can even help a minister's sense of vocation and pastoral identity. In 2004 Marilynne Robinson published *Gilead,* an epistolary novel that would win a Pulitzer Prize and a front-page celebratory review by James Wood in *The New York Times Book Review.* Remarkably, such high praise (there was an avalanche of it in big newspapers across the land) came to a novel about a quiet, small-town Christian minister, John Ames, who describes his sermon texts and tells how it feels to baptize a baby. It turns out that this 76-year-old man is full of grace and truth, but also of doubt and, for most of his life,

8. Garrett Keizer, *The Enigma of Anger: Essays on a Sometimes Deadly Sin* (San Francisco: Jossey-Bass, 2004).

9. Chiamanda Ngozi Adiechie, *Purple Hibiscus,* reprint ed. (Chapel Hill: Algonquin, 2012).

10. Daniel Goleman, *Vital Lies, Simple Truths: The Psychology of Self-Deception* (New York: Simon & Schuster, 1996).

11. Joseph Epstein has written that in *Sister Carrie* and especially in *An American Tragedy* Dreiser shows "he felt more deeply than anyone else what it was like to be an outsider and knew more about the heat of desire, of sheer human wanting than any man who ever wrote." Epstein, "A Literary Education," http://www.newcriterion.com/articles.cfm/A-literary-education-3855.

painful loneliness. He accepts that Scripture is a complex ancient literature and that, some of the time, it's tough to interpret. He pours himself into his sermons, "trying to say what was true" in them, but he is also serene in the knowledge that one day somebody will probably burn them.

Ames celebrates the sacrament of sheer existence in his church members, treating each as unrepeatable. Each, to him, is a unique and incandescent divine thought. His pastoral identity is secure enough to harbor within it a genial self-irony — which, to me, is an especially appealing species of humility. Ames tells us one of his dreams: "I was preaching to Jesus Himself, saying any foolish thing I could think of, and He was sitting there in His white, white robe looking patient and sad and amazed."[12]

John Ames is full of Scripture, but his last words in the novel are King Lear's: "I'll pray and then I'll sleep."

A wise practice, I believe, for this very night.

---

12. Robinson, *Gilead* (New York: Farrar, Straus, Giroux, 2004), p. 68.

Chapter 5

Wisdom on the Variousness of Life

I begin this chapter with four passages from fiction that all tend in a certain direction. The direction will come clear below. You may think that four examples right at the start of a chapter might be too many beads and not enough string and you may be right. But consider the mafia hit man Baglione in Stephen Vizinczey's novel titled *An Innocent Millionaire*.

Baglione "didn't see himself as a killer" because of all the people he had had in his power to kill, he had actually killed only nine. He had spared hundreds. He considered himself "a man of extraordinary restraint."[1] I am with Baglione. Of the hundreds of examples with which to start this chapter I am limiting myself to four, because I am a man of extraordinary restraint. I will even count Baglione as example 1.

My second example is from Victor Hugo. His masterpiece *Les Miserables* is a long story because Hugo veers off the road all the time on fascinating detours about anything that snags his interest including, for example, laziness, which Hugo describes as self-defeating. The lazy person resists work, resents work, obsesses about work, and so turns work into something twice

---

1. Stephen Vizinczey, *An Innocent Millionaire* (Boston: Atlantic Monthly, 1985), p. 187.

as unpleasant as it might otherwise have been if he had simply tackled it.[2]

Hugo is endlessly distracted, but he saw deeply into human life and never more than when drawing Jean Valjean's nemesis Javert. Jean Valjean, you may recall, is the protagonist of the novel. He is a powerful, deeply conflicted man, who is shaken so deeply by the grace of the godly priest Father Bienvenue that he becomes a good man, a believable good man — in fact one of the greatest depictions in fiction of a complicated good man. Valjean is all the more interesting and plausible to us because he is a man with a past.

He is also pursued by his past in the person of the police officer Javert, who has a list of Valjean's old crimes, real or imagined, and will not give up in his pursuit. That's because Javert is a legalist, a man earnest and austere in his righteousness, always awake, always watching. I have often thought of Javert in connection with Psalm 139. "You have searched me, Lord, and you know me. You know when I sit and when I rise."

If God is a relentless and merciless detective — always wakeful, always watchful — then no wonder, said Paul Tillich, that in every age there are people who want to murder God. "The God Who sees everything, and man also, is the God Who has to die. Man cannot stand that such a Witness live."[3]

Javert's sworn duty is to detect and penalize transgressions of the law. Hugo tells us that Javert "was a spy the way other men were priests." The law is Javert's god, so sacrosanct that the least violation of it, even by a man who steals a loaf of bread to feed hungry children, deserves nothing but contempt and punish-

---

2. Victor Hugo, *Les Miserables* (New York: Penguin, 1985), p. 793.
3. Paul Tillich, "Escape from God," http://www.godweb.org/shaking.htm.

ment. For Javert, this judgment is absolute. "God knows," he says, that "it's easy to be kind; the hard thing is to be just."[4]

In the end Javert is destroyed by grace. He catches Valjean, but in a shocking reversal, Valjean gets Javert at his mercy. He could kill him and be rid of his tormentor forever, but he doesn't do it. He lets Javert go. And this unexpected grace devastates Javert. For the first time he finds himself admiring a felon and cannot help it. A merciful lawbreaker in the universe? Hugo tells us that Javert "is forced to admit that this monstrosity could exist . . . a merciful lawbreaker in the universe" and that it tears Javert up "by the roots."[5]

Worse, Javert finds Valjean's kindness to be contagious. He feels an impulse rising in him to do as he has been done by, and, in the future, to let Valjean go. Horrified by this impulse, Javert concludes that he has sinned against his own integrity and that the only honorable course left to him now is suicide.

Voodoo and a Self-Appointed Durwan

Third example: in David Duncan's novel *The Brothers K* we find a family of baseball lovers, including especially Papa Chance, a mill worker who had hoped to be a professional baseball player. He never made it, but he still loved to tell his boys stories about baseball. At one point he tells them about Ted Williams, the great batting champion of the Boston Red Sox.

He tells them that Williams knew where the strike zone is. It's "wherever the umpire says it is."[6] The strike zone exists only

---

4. Hugo, *Les Miserables,* p. 200.
5. Hugo, *Les Miserables,* p. 1106.
6. David Duncan, *The Brothers K* (New York: Bantam, 1992), p. 132.

inside the umpire's head. Knowing this, Williams concocts a scheme. Though he would not usually give interviews he finally grants one interview to a minor reporter and answers all his questions truthfully till he gets the one question he wants: "How do you hit so good?'" Williams tells the reporter that he studies pitchers, that his concentration and mechanics and bat speed are all good. And then, at that point of the interview, Williams stares into the reporter's mousy eyes and says this:

> Everybody knows that there are quick wrists and slow wrists, but not many know that there are quick and slow eyes too. And my eyes . . . are the key to my hitting. They're my secret weapon. Because my eyes are so quick I can see any pitch, even a fastball, all the way in to where it jumps off my bat. . . .[7]

Well, said Papa Chance to his boys, "Umpires read the papers too, just like everybody else, and they bought it." In the next season, William's strike zone shrank to one square foot. If Williams took a pitch the umps assumed those quick eyes had *seen* that it was high or low or in or out. The plate's corners disappeared because no ump wanted to challenge Williams's "baby blues that saw in a fastball not a blur, but a hundred and eight scarlet stitches on four fat white cheeks." What Williams did to the umps was voodoo. "The next season Williams hit 400" all because "Williams' eyesight was good, but his voodoo was downright splendid."[8]

Fourth example: in 1999 Jhumpa Lahiri won the Pulitzer Prize for fiction with her debut collection of stories titled *Interpreter of Maladies*. No wonder. The stories delight, amuse, fasci-

7. Duncan, *The Brothers K*, p. 133.
8. Duncan, *The Brothers K*, p. 134.

nate. A number of them end sorrowfully enough to break your heart. The prose sings along simply and lyrically, never calling attention to itself, always calling attention to the music. Lahiri is like a concert violinist who doesn't care whether you go home saying, "What articulation! What a gorgeous tone!" The good violinists want you to go home saying, "Thank God for Prokofiev!"

Lahiri is an American of Bengali descent, born in London but raised in Rhode Island. Her stories are largely about the lives of Indian immigrants to the U.S. along several generations. They are deeply revealing. A couple of them are set in India, including one titled "A Real Durwan."9

A durwan in India is a doorkeeper, especially of an apartment building. In her story, Lahiri gives us Boori Ma, who is a kind of de facto durwan in an apartment building in Calcutta. She sleeps on a quilt or two under the apartment mailboxes, right at the entrance. The residents of the apartment building do not mind, particularly because, in exchange for her shelter, Boori Ma sweeps the stairs of the building.

Boori Ma is 64. She is shrill, arthritic, and full of stories about her prosperous life before she had been deported to Calcutta. She tells everybody how her bare feet never used to touch anything but marble, how her expensive linens comforted her, how the mayor attended the wedding of her third daughter, who was married amidst great opulence.

Boori Ma still has a ring of keys to all the coffer boxes that once held her valuables. These she has tied to the free end of her sari so that as she brooms the stairs and mumbles over her losses the keys clink together, reminding everybody of Boori Ma's splendid past.

9. Jhumpa Lahiri, "A Real Durwan," in her *Interpreter of Maladies: Stories* (Boston: Houghton Mifflin, 1999), pp. 70-82.

Mind you, none of the tenants in the building knows how much to *credit* Boori Ma's stories, but they accept her anyway because her stories entertain them and because she is wonderful on the stairs with her broom. One more thing: because Boori Ma used to preside over a substantial estate, as she claims, she takes it upon herself to preside now over the entrance to the apartment building. She patrols the activities there, screening the peddlers, summoning rickshaws, routing vagrants who eye the entrance to the building as a spot to spit or pee. And any time the tenants of the apartment get irritated with Boori Ma's clinking keys and doubtful tales, they recall that for a self-appointed durwan, she is pretty good at her job.

Then comes the turn in the story. One of the apartment residents comes into some money and installs a sink in his apartment. In a burst of generosity he then buys one for the communal use of the rest of the building. Barefoot plumbers install the sink, and the donor invites all the tenants to use it. They're delighted, because for years they had brushed their teeth with saved-up water stored in mugs.

Boormi Ma is unimpressed. She looks at the new sink and sniffs. "Our bathwater [used to be] scented with petals and attars," she says. "Believe me, don't believe me, it was a luxury you cannot dream."[10]

In unexpected ways the sink becomes a source of resentment, rumor, and a sequence of events that catches Boori Ma up in them and pits her against the tenants, who start clamoring for a real durwan to replace their self-appointed one.

As Lahiri tells it, the story sticks in the memory. It gives us a woman who is surprisingly good with a broom for someone who used to have servants. She presides regally over the

10. Lahiri, "A Real Durwan," pp. 78-79.

entrance to a poor apartment building because of her experience, maybe imaginary, of having presided over an estate. The story centers memorably on how a single piece of plumbing becomes a curse in the lives of people who had welcomed it as a blessing.

Along the way, we get surprised by the familiar in exotic places. In a poor apartment building in Calcutta we find status and shame, gratitude and resentment, dreams of old glory, and doubt aroused by stories too good to be true. In the alley outside the apartment building in Calcutta, 8-year-old boys play cops and robbers as they might anywhere in the world.

Not as Simple as You Think

So we have Baglione, the hit man proud of his restraint; Javert, devastated by grace; Ted Williams, whose voodoo was even better than his eyesight; and Boori Ma, whose keys on the end of her sari clink with glory and shame.

Why would a preacher want to read about these characters?

As a preacher, the reason I want to read about Baglione, Javert, Ted Williams, and Boori Ma is that each one surprises me. Each pulls at my imagination and expands it. Each character reminds me that life is more various and mysterious than I had imagined and that it will not stay inside the bright lines I have drawn for it.

In one of his many terrific essays, Joseph Epstein writes about this. Citing Milan Kundera, Epstein reminds us that good literature always complicates. "The novelist says to the reader: things are not as simple as you think . . . life is more surprising, bizarre, fascinating, complex, and rich than any shibboleth, concept, or theory used to explain it." In reading good writers we get "a strong taste for the . . . variousness of life; . . . how astonishing reality is and how obdurate to even the most ingenious attempts to grasp its mechanics or explain any serious portion of it!"[11]

As a preacher, I want my shibboleths challenged because I am as vulnerable to dogmatic myopia as anybody, and if I peddle my dogmatic myopia from the pulpit I subvert the richer understandings of life within the gospel and disqualify myself as a responsible minister of it.

Take just one example: as a preacher I need to be wary of social and cultural dogmatisms in speaking of personal identity and of the good life that depends on getting my identity straight. It is too easy here to be sucked into a prevailing fashion, as Robert Schuller was back in the 1970s by adopting self-esteem as an important part of human thriving and then the most important part. By the 1980s Schuller published a book in which he explicitly stated that self-esteem is identical with salvation and that his insight about it constituted what he called "the New Reformation."[12]

Here is exactly where somebody needed to say, "Wait a minute. Things are not as simple as you think." "Wait a minute. *Baglione* had high self-esteem."

As a preacher I need to be wary of current dogmatisms about personal identity. People keep peddling fashionable ideas of it and the well-read preacher will have thought about them. David Wells once listed some of the main contenders. Who am I? "I am my genes; I am my past; I am my sexual orientation; I am my feel-

11. Joseph Epstein, "A Literary Education," http://www.newcriterion.com/articles.cfm/A-literary-education-3855.

12. Robert Schuller, *Self-Esteem: The New Reformation* (Waco, TX: Word, 1982). Worried that a conflation of self-esteem and salvation might tempt people to give in to egotism? Never mind, Schuller wrote, since "the Cross will sanctify your ego trip" just as it did for Jesus (pp. 74-75).

ings; I am my image; I am my body; I am what I do; I am what I have; I am who I know."[13]

These self-identifications have competing anthropologies behind them, and none will look very good to a serious Christian — at least not until they have been significantly reframed inside a Christian understanding of the human person.

In any case, for most fixed ideas of how to explain personal identity, or human motivation, or freedom and responsibility, or the longing for God, or the meaning of life, I want my basic Christian commitments to challenge and qualify these fixed ideas, and I want my program of reading to help me.

Joseph Epstein, once more:

> From the study of literature we learn that life is sad, comic, heroic, vicious, dignified, ridiculous, and endlessly amusing sometimes by turns, sometimes all at once, but never more grotesquely amusing than when a supposedly great thinker comes along to insist that he has discovered and nattily formulated the single key to its understanding.[14]

Epstein is thinking of Sigmund Freud, whose "extreme determinism" seems "immensely untrue to the rich complexity of life, with its twists and turns and manifold surprises."[15]

As a preacher I want to read about Baglione and Javert and Ted Williams and Boori Ma because they surprise me. They remind me how remorselessly parochial I am, peering out at life from my single point of view and trying to stuff everything I see into my prefabricated categories. The good writers make me dis-

---

13. Wells, *Losing Our Virtue: Why the Church Must Recover Its Moral Vision* (Grand Rapids: Eerdmans, 1998), p. 141.

14. Epstein, "A Literary Education."

15. Epstein, "A Literary Education."

cover how hopeless it is to keep on stuffing in this way and there is liberation in the discovery.

Yet the good writers do not confound my understanding of life completely. After reading them I do retain some islands of stability within the high seas of variability. The hit man Baglione may surprise me that he prides himself on his restraint, but it does not surprise me that he wants to appear right in his own eyes. Javert may surprise me by being horrified at his impulse to show kindness to Jean Valjean, but only because his horror is an extravagantly *consistent* example of legalism, and legalism doesn't surprise me. Ted Williams's voodoo surprises me because I hadn't thought of the possibility that a hitter could reach into an umpire's brain and squeeze the strike zone there, but the hunger to gain an edge by manipulating people is ubiquitous and doesn't surprise me. Boori Ma's self-appointment as durwan based on her experience of presiding over an estate has a poignancy that moves and surprises me, but her need to have a little area over which she has her say, her need to have a small personal kingdom, doesn't surprise me in the least, because her need is part of the image of God in us, as old and deep as creation itself.

Surprises in the preacher's general reading are the raisins in the oatmeal. They lie in material that is unsurprising, which is a good thing because it makes our reading intelligible. If everything in our reading were a novelty we would be disquieted, to say the least. We would be like a person who has been through a botched eyelid lift. The plastic surgeon was way too aggressive and so his patient now walks in the world wearing a look of perpetual astonishment.

The preacher wants his program of reading to complicate some of his fixed ideas, to impress him with some of the mysteries of life, with its variousness, with its surprises, with the pushes and pulls within it. If not before, preachers will then know as well as anyone how often life makes us want to laugh and cry at the same time.

God's Other Name

None of this changes when it comes to life with God. As a confessionally Reformed Christian I believe in the faithfulness of God, the providence of God, the immutability of God's nature. Reformed Christianity is not a cult, so I share my faith in God's sovereign reliability with all two billion of the rest of us Christians. But I have lived long enough and read widely enough and listened to Walter Brueggemann often enough to know that, besides reliability, "God's other name is surprise."[16]

This is quite often so when it comes to God's providence, and our preacher's reading will give him multiple examples. Take the story of Victor Klemperer.[17] Klemperer was professor of literature at the University of Dresden in the years that led into World War II, and he had the job he wanted. All his life he had loved to read and write, and all his adult life he had dreamed of writing the world's best book on eighteenth-century French literature. If he succeeded, he could hold his head up in the faculty lounge. In fact, he would be known on campuses across the world. At conferences he could autograph his book, and he could do it graciously and illegibly. He would be a master in his field. Anybody who wanted to talk about eighteenth-century French literature would have to talk about Viktor Klemperer.

16. A favorite observation of my colleague Dale Cooper, former Chaplain of Calvin College.

17. Victor Klemperer, *I Will Bear Witness: A Diary of the Nazi Years,* 2 vols., vol. 1: *1933-1941;* vol. 2: *1942-1945,* trans. Martin Chalmers (New York: Random House, 1998-99).

But then the Nazis came to power and started removing one part of Klemperer's life after another. They took away his telephone and then his car. They cancelled some of his courses at the University, and then they cancelled all of them. The Nazis removed his typewriter and then they took away his house and gave it to a local grocer. (The grocer, by the way, was actually opposed to Hitler, but he was still pleased to have Klemperer's house.) The Nazis moved Klemperer into a so-called Jews' House, which was normally the last stop on the way to the camps, and they also killed Klemperer's cat because, of course, Jews could not own pets.

As the Nazis robbed him, Klemperer wrote it all down in his diary. He wrote about his deprivations and the indignities that came with them. He described suffering and what it did to people — how it made some of them large-hearted and compassionate and how it made others tight and self-protective. In May of 1942, after a terrifying house search by the Gestapo, which always included vandalism and beatings even of the elderly, Klemperer wrote in his diary that if his diary were discovered he would be killed. "But I shall go on writing . . . I will bear witness, precise witness."[18] He knew that in his confinement he couldn't write a big history of Nazi cruelty. But he could tell his diary about the ordinary ways that the Nazis stripped people of their dignity, right down to the last tattered bit of it.

Viktor Klemperer had hoped to write the world's best account of eighteenth-century French literature. But the Nazis took his life away.

Except that, at the end of the day, they didn't. They couldn't. The reason is that Viktor Klemperer and his diary survived and are now celebrated all over the world. Victor Klemperer's diary is

18. Klemperer, *I Will Bear Witness*, vol. 2, p. 61.

his distinction. It's what he is known for. Klemperer had thought that his glory would be a book about French literature, but the Lord meant his daily diary to be his glory.[19] Klemperer could not stop the Nazis from robbing him, but there was one thing he *could* do. He could "bear witness, precise witness," and he could bear it to the end. He was a witness to the truth, and he did not know that this would be his glory. He was like Moses coming down the mountain from God with his face shining, except that Moses didn't *know* his face was shining.

God is great and God is good, but God is also elusive and unpredictable. Kathleen Norris comments on this in her book of observations on faith titled *Amazing Grace*.[20] In Exodus 3 Moses is attracted to a burning bush, and God calls to him from it, "Moses! Moses!" And Moses said, " 'Here I am.' "

Then God gives Moses an intimidating assignment. Moses is to go to Pharaoh and tell him his oppression of the Israelites is over now because Moses will be liberating them. "So now, go," says God. "I'm sending you to Pharaoh." "But Moses says to God, 'Who am I that I should go to Pharaoh?' And God says, 'I will be with you' and here's the sign of it: 'Once you have delivered the Israelites out of Pharaoh's hand, you will all worship me on this very mountain.' "

Kathleen Norris comments that God can be known in our calling, but the scary thing is that sometimes we know it was God calling us only after we have completed whatever it is that God calls us to.[21] Moses will know that it was actually God who

---

19. My friend Eleonore Stump gave me this insight and pointed me to the Klemperer diary.

20. Kathleen Norris, *Amazing Grace: A Vocabulary of Faith* (New York: Riverhead, 1998).

21. Norris, *Amazing Grace*, p. 110.

called him only when he actually has the Israelites with him on the mountain.

OK, says Moses, but meanwhile the people are going to want your name. If I tell them that the God of their ancestors has sent me to them, they're going to ask, "What is his name?"

Norris writes: "The next passage might be seen as the premiere of Jewish humor, an exchange from a Borscht Belt stage in the 40s. 'What is your name?' Moses asks, and God says, 'I am who I am.'" Norris comments: "Moses might as well have asked, 'Who's on first?'"[22]

Our preacher could read Thomas Aquinas on Exodus 3:14 and get some of the finest theology ever written on God's essence and existence and the simplicity that makes them the same thing. But he could also read Kathleen Norris, and be reminded that before Moses or anybody gets within a mile of God's essence and existence, before the theology could begin to be written, or the reverence before God's self-revelation could begin to develop, the first thing to notice is that the sentence "I am who I am" sounds initially less like a name than a vaudeville line.

God is great and God is good, but God is also elusive and unpredictable, and the preacher's reading can help him see this. My own introduction to the mysteries of petitionary prayer came to me as a boy while reading *Huckleberry Finn*. In the third chapter Huck tells us that Miss Watson had taught him to pray, promising that whatever he asked for, he would get it.

"But it warn't so," says Huck.

I tried it. Once I got a fish line but no hooks. It warn't any good to me without hooks. I tried for the hooks three or four times but somehow I couldn't make it work. By and by, one day I

22. Norris, *Amazing Grace*, p. 111.

asked Miss Watson to try for me, but she said I was a fool. She never told me why and I couldn't make it out no way.[23]

God is un-guessable. We can tell from the wild variety of images for God in Scripture itself. In his book titled *The Iconoclastic Deity*,[24] Clyde Holbrook reminds us that in Scripture God is not only a leopard, eagle, and bear, but also a moth; not only a fortress, lamp, and rock, but also dry rot. Everybody knows that the Bible portrays God as king, judge, shepherd, lord, father, and mother. But the Bible also portrays God as an archer, vintner, watchman, barber, and whistler. For all of us who think biblical images of God represent not just human speculation, but also God's self-revelation, some of these images carry a wonderful tinge of divine self-irony.

Poignance of the Incarnation

Jesus, too, is both knowable and hard to know, both reliable and un-guessable. Once our preacher has got in the habit of finding unpredictability in God he will spot it in the Son of God too. Every so often the gospels themselves show us a little of the unlikelihood of the incarnation by suggesting that divinity and humanity are a difficult combination.

One day (Mark 8:22-26) some people bring a blind man to Jesus and beg for his healing touch. Jesus has the divine power so he doesn't shrink from the job, and Jesus has Godly love all the way down to his generous heart, so he wants to *do* the job. He takes

23. Mark Twain, *The Adventures of Huckleberry Finn*, http://classiclit.about
.com/library/bl-etexts/mtwain/bl-mtwain-huck-3.htm.
24. Clyde A. Holbrook, *The Iconoclastic Deity: Biblical Images of God* (Lewisburg: Bucknell University Press, 1984).

the blind man by the hand (what tenderness!) and leads him outside town. Then Jesus goes to work. Mark says plainly that Jesus spits in this man's eyes. In Mark 8 we are only one chapter beyond Mark's story of Jesus spitting on his finger and then touching the tongue of a man who cannot talk. He touches this man's tongue with the fingered spit.

We mortals generally cannot do much for blindness or muteness. Jesus can because he is God but Jesus spits all the time because he's also a blue-collar man of the first century. How familiar the love is and how strange the process is. It seems we can know Jesus, but he is hard to know.

And the story has an even more remarkable turn. Jesus lays hands on the blind man, and then asks him a simple question: "Do you see anything?"

"Do you see anything?" All heaven's power and love in the healing touch of the Son of God, except that it's the Son of God incarnate who has a very human touch. He *thinks* he has just healed the blindness, but to be sure he asks this almost boyish question. Did it work? Did I get it? "Do you see anything?"

Not quite says the blind man. I can see people, OK, but they all "look like trees walking around." And so Jesus, who has emptied himself to share our lot, gamely goes at the blindness a second time. And then, after a double try, the healing works and the man sees and the action moves on.

I find this one of the most moving stories about Jesus in the Bible. It is so revealing of the metaphysical leakage at the joint where God and man are welded together in the incarnation. The story seems so poignant and so revealing of the fact that we cannot begin to understand what is involved in getting a divine person, the eternal Son of God, actually enfleshed.

Where blindness is concerned, God can do anything. Where blindness is concerned, a human being cannot do anything.

Where blindness is concerned the incarnate Son of God can pull it off, maybe, but it's very tricky, so he asks a half-eager, half-doubtful question: "Do you see anything?"

The late Donald Juel, who taught New Testament at Princeton Theological Seminary with great distinction, used to teach his students to approach every preachable text in the interrogative mood. Ask the text everything you can think of, including about the tone of voice of the speakers in the text. "Do you see anything?" Or imagine Jesus speaking to the Phoenician woman in Mark 7: "It is not right to take the children's bread and toss it to the dogs." How would Jesus have said these hard words to that poor woman? Maybe with a tone that signals an inside joke? Or think of the Roman centurion in Mark 15 after seeing how Jesus died with a loud cry. The centurion says "Surely this man was the Son of God," which is one of the bookends in Mark. But how did the centurion say the words? Lost in wonder, love, and praise? Or still in mocking mode?

The centurion of Mark 15 has humiliated Jesus in the most effective way possible, namely by crucifixion, which took Jesus' life, but before that, took his dignity. At the end Jesus cries out and then he dies. His light goes out. Did the centurion, watching with a veteran's eye, chuckle to himself? "Sure, this man was the Son of God all right, except that right now he's one dead son of god."

Redrawing the Lines

"The spirit of the novel is the spirit of complexity," writes Milan Kundera. "The novelist says to the reader, 'Things are not as simple you think.'" Preachers need the message, because naïve preaching is a kind of malpractice. The wise preacher sticks with his reading program to become wiser not only about the variousness of life, but also about some of the wonders within it. Naïveté is often the child of ignorance, but wonder is often the child of *imagination.*

In his novel *Mariette in Ecstasy* Ron Hansen tells a story of Mariette Baptiste, a beautiful and pious young woman who enters the priory of The Sisters of Crucifixion as a postulant. The setting is upstate New York in 1906. Everything in the priory is ordered. One sister makes the candles; another makes the wine. One is the gardener and one is the milkmaid. Each has a precise responsibility, and all owe obedience to the prioress.

Each day begins at precisely 2 a.m. with the "first rising" in silence, and every hour thereafter is assigned for recitation, meditation, private prayer, meals, work, or saying the offices of the day. The sisters may only sleep on their beds and only at night. At other times they may not sit on them, weep on them, or pray on them. Beds are for sleeping.

Within this regimented life Mariette is a distraction. She is, after all, new, young, and radiantly beautiful. She is also — according to her own father, a physician — given to "trances, hallucinations, unnatural piety, great extremes of temperament, and 'inner wrenchings.'"[25] When Mariette begins to bleed from her hands and feet and side, from visible stigmata, the priory goes berserk. Mariette speaks demurely of these "gifts," but half the priory thinks the wounds are self-inflicted, or marks of the devil, or products of Mariette's hysteria.

The reading preacher notes anew that the gifted always attract difficult forms of attention, including being accused of wanting attention. But there is another thread in the weave. The novelist hints that Mariette has been sexually abused by her father, and the reader, connecting the dots, begins to wonder. Do victims of sexual

25. Ron Hansen, *Mariette in Ecstasy* (New York: E. Burlingame, 1991), p. 31.

abuse create an alternative reality to which they may escape, and has Mariette done this by fabricating stigmata? Or does God sometimes *grant* victims of sexual abuse an alternative reality to which they may escape, and has God done this for Mariette?[26]

So artful is Hansen's ambiguity as to the authenticity of Mariette's stigmata that the reader is left in a state of perfect ambivalence, which is the takeaway from the novel. To the preacher this ambivalence is gift and calling. He may have heard miracle tales it was impossible to judge. He may have heard reports that began "the Lord said to me" and wondered how to respond. The Bible itself is full of dreams, visions, miracles, angel visits, instances of God speaking.

Meanwhile, like everybody else the preacher lives in a world describable and predictable by scientists, who know in advance what time the sun will come up and who have natural descriptions of everything significant. So, like everybody else, the preacher's sense of the world flattens out and his expectations become tame and domestic. Even his denomination's publishing arm describes Jesus' "miracle of feeding the 5,000" in natural terms as a "miracle" of generosity. It seems that enough of the 5,000 had enough food with them for all and were inspired to share!

Periodically, what the preacher wants is somebody like Hansen to upset his sense of where the lines of reality are drawn and to make him wonder all over again about the mighty hand of God in the world. The Bible is a supernatural book with a supernatural story of creation and redemption done by a supernatural God. Preachers without supernatural understandings and expectations end up preaching a tiny gospel about a disappointingly skinny God.

Even when fiction is non-religious, it can help the preacher

---

26. I owe the thought in these last two sentences to some intelligent person, but have lost the reference.

loosen up his worldview enough to admit into it strange objects of wonder. This is especially true of literary fantasy and of science fiction, including for young people. The main reason C. S. Lewis and J. R. R. Tolkien are household names is that their fantasies grab and hold the attention of the younger members of the household. From 1997 to 2007 J. K. Rowling published seven novels featuring a youthful wizard named Harry Potter and the books became sensations all over the world, inspiring millions. Publishers marveled that middle-schoolers were toting and reading lengthy books, sometimes postponing favorite activities so they could get their head back in Rowling. One reason is that Rowling knew the lure of a fantasy world, in which things happen that no imagination had previously conceived.

Ray Bradbury, the author of *Fahrenheit 451,* wrote a great many short stories. People call some of them science fiction, but Bradbury liked to call them fantasy, and some of them instill a sense of the numinous. We usually think of the sense of the numinous as a sense of God's overpowering otherness, the combined majesty and awfulness of God that makes us shudder and shrink before it. But in Bradbury's stories there is also a sense of the numinous about creation, which is seldom as simple as we think.

So in a famous story called "The Fog Horn"[27] two men shiver in a lighthouse on a cold November evening when the mist is heavy enough that they have set the fog horn to blow every fifteen seconds. They are discussing the mysteries of the sea, and the voice of the fog horn calling to the sea — the fog horn which makes a sound so lonesome that "whoever hears it will weep in their souls," because now they know "the sadness of eternity and the briefness of life."

27. Ray Bradbury, "The Fog Horn," http://www.grammarpunk.com/lit/gp/THE_FOG_HORN.pdf.

As the men talk, a creature's head surfaces in the sea just within range of their light, and then the neck emerges and more neck and still more till forty feet of neck tower up, tall as the lighthouse itself, and the creature's great lantern eyes turn to the top of the lighthouse and begin to reflect its light. The eyes of the monster with the light flashing back from them become disks "sending a message in primeval code."

The dinosaurs died out a million years ago, but here's one now rising from the deeps where it had sequestered itself, rising to the sight of the light and the sound of the horn. It seems to recognize the lighthouse as a lost love — the lighthouse with its forty-foot neck and shining light and mournful call.

> The fog horn blew and the monster answered. [Its] cry came across a million years of water and mist. A cry so anguished and alone that it made [the two men] shudder. The fog horn blew. The monster cried again. The fog horn blew. The monster opened its great toothed mouth and the sound that came from it was the sound of the fog horn itself. Lonely and vast and far away.

"It was the sound of one who had waited a million years for the voice of the lighthouse to call [it home]."[28]

After reading Bradbury, our preacher cannot think of Scripture's "sea monsters" or "monsters of the deep" without wondering if any have a cry that is "lonely and vast and far away." Once again, our preacher's program of reading has opened doors in him he did not know he had.

---

28. Bradbury, "The Fog Horn."

Chapter 6

Wisdom on Sin and Grace

A preacher needs to be a sage in order to speak responsibly from the pulpit week by week. She has to have something worth listening to on some of the mightiest subjects in the world, including how the universe looks to a Christian, who human beings are, the human predicament, God's gracious address to the predicament in Jesus Christ, the resulting prognosis for our world, and, along the way, much, much else. Fortunately, she has our community's book to draw from, which is wonderful except that she now has to bridge from Scripture, which is a multiplex ancient literature, to her own particular context and engage an audience there that is certain to be mixed in some formidable ways.

The preacher has to be a little crazy to tackle all this. Or else, like the Apostle Paul, she needs to have seen the risen Lord. In either case, once embarked, the preacher will need to get wisdom with all deliberate speed.

Wisdom isn't all we want in our preachers, of course. We're looking for integrity as well and a hunger for justice. We'd like to see godliness without stuffiness and a love of Scripture and a lively empathy where others are concerned. A devout prayer life would seem essential, too, and an expansive vision of the Kingdom of God. In other words, the Apostle Paul on a good day.

One more thing: part of the standard equipment on a preacher has got to be a fairly lively sense of humor. It's a healthy part of social intelligence and a delightful leaven within a sermon. I grew up amongst West Michigan Calvinists, who are a sturdy people. But we were Calvinists of Northern European extraction and formal in worship, so humor in our pulpits was rare and unintended. The best we could hope for was the occasional spoonerism ("So let us live for the Lord with renewed veal and zigor" or the bonanza spoonerism to 9-year-old ears, namely, a mess up on "Satan's fiery darts"). Once my boyhood minister wanted to say that "sin is like a worm, gnawing from within," but what he actually said was that "sin is like a gnaw, worming from within." Most of our folks got the idea just fine that way.

My boyhood preachers were honest and Godly men, but they would have thought deliberate humor in the pulpit to be impertinent, and in both senses of the word. It would have been disrespectful and it would have been irrelevant. They had other business of a Sunday morning. Reformed doctrine needed to be preached. Eternal destinies needed to be secured. The Kuyperian vision of the Kingdom of God needed to be hammered home. It was all terribly earnest and it included one big advantage: my boyhood preachers never compromised on sin and grace. In fact, the grace of God overwhelmed them just because they saw and preached the devastating effects of sin.

A lot on this front has changed, and I'll write more about it below.

Meanwhile, a lot of us these days do want a sense of humor in our preacher and preferably one that's not too eccentric. You don't really want it to show up on Good Friday, for instance, and you don't want your preacher to strain when it comes to amusing the congregation. If at some point in the sermon the preacher says, "Well, folks, all kidding aside," you want that to follow actual laughter. If there wasn't any laughter, you don't want your preacher to explain why there should have been. In any case — always, always — we want our preacher's laughter to contain some dimension of kindness and understanding.

I believe that generous laughter of this sort is nowadays almost a prophetic witness. So much public laughter has an edge. Laugh lines on the campaign trail trigger derision and are meant to. Radio talk show hosts turn quickly to mockery — of people, not just of their positions. TV reality shows too often include or invite belittling.

Wisdom about Sin and Shame

Or think of middle school bullying, which usually includes mockery. Part of what makes it hurt is that much of it today is online. Jeers aimed at a 13-year-old girl now become a semi-public humiliation. Bad enough that she can read her humiliation, but so can her classmates and cousins and the kid next door who starts to look at her differently. Online bullying may injure a young spirit in ways that loving parents feel helpless to repair. Even back in the day when school mockery was more local, it hurt terribly.

I often think in this connection of a passage in W. Somerset Maugham. Near the start of his novel titled *Of Human Bondage* the 9-year-old Philip Carey enters King's School, Tercanbury, and discovers that it is a house of torment. Philip has talipes which, back in the day, people used to call clubfoot. In any case, Philip's unusual foot fascinates the other boys and turns them into mimics. On his second day at school, the other boys bring Philip into their game of "Pig in the Middle" during recess. Pig in the Middle turns out to be a playground game in which one boy roves in the center of the playground as all of the other boys dash across it. If the rover catches one of them, then, of course, there's a new pig in the middle for the next round of the game.

The boys make Philip pig in the middle from the start and it's a disaster. He can't catch anybody. His foot doesn't work for a game like this no matter how desperately he tries. Worse, after watching Philip struggle, one of his classmates gets the brilliant idea of mimicking him by clumping across the middle of the playground with just the right combination of awkwardness and quickness so as both to mock Philip and elude him. This spectacle sets off the others. Soon they are all limping and hooting their way past Philip, "screaming in their treble voices," as they drag one foot and then the other.[1]

That night in the dormitory, a boy named Singer approaches Philip to make a request: "I say, let's look at your foot." When Philip refuses, jumping into bed instead and balling up the bedclothes around his legs, Singer calls for another boy and the two of them pin Philip's arm and twist it. They ask again: "Why don't you show us your foot quietly?"[2] After a third boy appears, adding more pressure, a horrified Philip finally thrusts his foot out from underneath the covers. The three boys then take their time to inspect it, remarking how peculiar it looks, how "beastly." Singer touches it with the tip of one finger, tracing the outline of the deformity, treating the foot as if it were a thing apart from Philip.

When the headmaster unexpectedly appears, the boys scamper back into their own cubicles and Philip turns his face into his pillow, clamping it with his teeth in order to contain his storming soul. Maugham says this: "He was crying not for the pain they had caused him, nor for the humiliation he had suffered when they looked at his foot, but with rage at himself because, unable to stand the torture, he had put out his foot of his own accord."[3]

1. W. Somerset Maugham, *Of Human Bondage* (New York: Bantam, 1991), p. 37.

2. Maugham, *Of Human Bondage*, p. 38.

3. Maugham, *Of Human Bondage*, p. 39.

Philip Carey was ashamed of his foot, but he was even more ashamed of having shown it. As a 9-year-old human being, he already had enough core in his character to think that by participating in his own humiliation he had thrown off the last rag of his dignity.

The preacher who reads Somerset Maugham can get some wisdom about sin and especially about the sin of mockery. For one thing, she will be reinforced in her knowledge that the young are capable of appalling cruelty. Where do they get it? Do they imitate the mean kids they know, maybe older schoolmates? Or, as the Heidelberg Catechism says, are they simply "born sinners, corrupt from conception on"?[4] Or, short of utter corruption in the crib, do they nonetheless have a disposition to sin that lies largely dormant until certain environmental or emotional factors stimulate it? How much moral power does a young person have to resist this stimulus, and how does his own free will come into play? Or isn't his will really free? But if it isn't, how can he be reproached for his cruelty?

You would almost think that smart theologians must have discovered the problem of moral responsibility inside bondage of the will and then written about it at some point in the history of the church.

Today's wise preacher will acquaint herself with contemporary versions of the problem. If she reads Arts & Letters Daily, a terrific online resource for articles, essays, columns, and reviews, or if she reads the *New York Review of Books,* she will find that cognitive neuroscientists are constantly chewing on the same bone as Pelagius and Augustine did, except that the raw data for the discussion now come from competing claims about the evolution of the human brain. If certain bad behaviors once had survival value — or

4. Answer 7.

are believed to have once had survival value — what if anything follows from this about human freedom and responsibility?

The preacher who reads Somerset Maugham ponders youthful sin, original sin, the stubborn mystery of sin. Also what Reinhold Niebuhr used to write about sinners in groups — how they will do things together they wouldn't have dreamed of doing if they had been alone.[5] How loyalty to the pack and fear of opposing its leaders may prevent even the decent from objecting to its cruelties. Which boy in the dormitory had the guts to push Singer off Philip's bed and tell him to leave the new boy alone? When Germany fell into the hands of a band of criminals, who had the guts to stand against the pack and its leader, and what happened to those who did?

The preacher with her head in Somerset Maugham thinks about youthful sin and group cruelty. She may gain a little wisdom about laughter too. She may be reminded of something she had once read (was it in Dante, maybe, or in Milton?), namely, that laughter changes its tone within different contexts so that just as there is the laughter of heaven so also there is the laughter of hell. The laughter of heaven is all joy and acclamation, with so much delight in it and genuine merriment, but the laughter of hell is all hooting and jeering and cat calls. In heaven the morning stars sing together and all the children of God shout for joy. In hell they pick out what is shameful about you and point at it. Then they mimic it. Then they all "scream in their treble voices."

In telling the story of Philip Carey in King's School, Somerset Maugham tells us preachers about old sins in young people, about the cruelty of groups, about the laughter of hell. *All this in one passage from a novel.* Yet another powerful current runs through the playground and cubicle scenes. I'm thinking of *shame,* one of the

5. Especially in *Moral Man and Immoral Society.*

most profound of human emotions and one of the most potent. Human shame is a feeling of distress at our deficiencies, deformities, or absurdities, and especially at the uncovering of these things. It is also a feeling of distress at the uncovering of our mere privacies. At the heart of shame lies a painful sense of having been exposed. Our poor, vulnerable self, which is foolish or guilty or homely or stupid or fat or merely private, gets undraped before the eyes of others and, crucially, before our own eyes, and the result is that we want to flee, to hide, to pull the bedclothes over us. In the worst cases we want to die: we want the mountains to fall on us and the hills to cover us. This may be especially likely in those cases, such as Philip Carey's, in which our shame arises from multiple sources — social unacceptability and exposure and guilt all layered on top of dismay over one's disfigurement.

The story of Philip Carey at King's School sticks to the preacher's soul not only because Maugham understood youthful sin and group sin and the laughter of hell and the shame of the vulnerable. The story sticks to the preacher also because it makes her *feel* keenly. As we noted earlier in the book, that's part of the artistry of the great writers. They know the way to our hearts. And so with Maugham's story. It may tend to make the preacher wiser, but also richer in tender mercies and fiercer in her hatred of sin and her longing for justice.

Hollywood Wiser Than Some Preachers?

Would these fine traits be superfluous in a preacher these days? Haven't we just had decades of no-fault morality in North America, and haven't the churches too often caved in the face of it? There is today little confession of sin in morning worship, even in conservative West Michigan. That act is just about gone. In many settings there is little place for the psalms of lament or self-accusation. Who these days can even understand Psalm 51, with its heartsick confession of sin and defilement, with its desperate plea for restoration?

And, of course, the biblical sense of sin and of grace go together, so that when the sense of sin decays in our churches so does the sense of grace. If even the *word* "sin" sounds trivial or quaint, then why would we still talk about grace? What would be the point?

David Wells has written five books on the topic — five books whose message is that evangelical religion in North America has lost its soul.[6] In too many churches today, says Prof. Wells, the only theology around is one in which "God is on easy terms" with popular culture and so is interested chiefly in church growth and psychological wholeness. Prof. Wells wants to know what St. Paul would make of evangelical churches — he of the cosmic Christology, and the rock-ribbed assurance of justification through faith, and the urgent summons to die and rise with Jesus Christ. What would St. Paul make of worship without lament, of pelvic-thrusting praise teams and beaming ministers on their barstools, swapping stories and jokes with an applauding audience and announcing "top ten" listings borrowed from Letterman?

The Babylonian captivity of the church to popular culture is too often true and always tragic.

And yet. How about the parents of a boy who has been relentlessly bullied in school and mocked online? Do they doubt the reality of sin or their child's need of mercy? What about women whose men belittle them, or cheat on them, or beat them and

---

6. *No Place for Truth* (1994), *God in the Wasteland* (1995), *Losing Our Virtue* (1999), *Above All Earthly Pow'rs* (2006), and *The Courage to Be Protestant* (2008) — all published by Eerdmans.

then accuse them of having triggered the beating? A man will beat a woman and then accuse her: "See what you made me do?"

How about a middle-aged man who has lost his job not to automation or to outsourcing or to necessary downsizing but to corporate politics driven largely by envy and greed? When a 48-year-old man feels emasculated, when nobody so much as acknowledges receipt of his job resumes and inquiries, when it looks as if he and his loved ones might lose the family home and his children simply cannot handle the downshift in the family's happiness, what do you think this man understands? Do you think a man cheated out of his job understands the old Christian categories of sin, corruption, misery, lament? How about the grace of God to heal and restore?

I believe a lot of ordinary people still do understand these things even if their ministers aren't supplying the biblical vocabulary for them. Maybe their minister won't talk to them about sin and grace so maybe they ought to talk to their minister about these realities. Tell their minister it's OK to talk about sin and grace and to do it right in church.

Are these concepts outdated? I don't think so. Look around town. Today, as always, middle-aged daughters struggle to forgive their mom who was never really a mom to them. People lose their savings to pious fraud and taste their deprivation every day. Inspectors get bribed not to inspect, and so cranes fall over on a downtown street. Comedians mock and jeer and sometimes they mock God and people find it mighty entertaining. Great nations launch costly wars against little nations, as the U.S. did in Vietnam. At least two Presidents were willing to sacrifice more and more lives on both sides to a war they knew was unwinnable *because they did not want to appear weak.*

All over the world, the stories pile up. Churches that silence the biblical message of sin and grace simply aren't anywhere near where people actually live their lives, including the kids in the congregation. Kids who read Harry Potter know all about good and evil. Maybe they wouldn't use the word "sin" to describe the evil in the books. Fine. Bracket the word "sin" and talk about what Voldemort does, what the Dementors do. Hollywood screenwriters are so conscious of good and evil that if a character cheats on a good woman or kills an innocent person, something will happen to him. He won't simply get away with it. The formula today is the same as it always has been: let dramatically portrayed evil entertain us, and then punish it satisfyingly before the end of the show. Do this because, of course, the guilty deserve to be punished. Hollywood writers are old-fashioned people. They mostly don't go to church so they have never learned that personal guilt for wrongdoing has become *passé*.

Pulitzer, O'Connor, Steinbeck

A preacher who wants wisdom about sin has lots of places to get it. For sheer information, one excellent source is www.pulitzer .org, the website of the Pulitzer Prizes, where years of investigative reporting are available to read. Here's a sample from the prizes won in the last eight years for investigative journalism:

> 2004 Awarded to **Michael D. Sallah, Mitch Weiss and Joe Mahr** of *The Blade,* Toledo, Ohio, for their powerful series on atrocities by Tiger Force, an elite U.S. Army platoon, during the Vietnam War.
>
> 2005 Awarded to **Nigel Jaquiss** of *Willamette Week,* Portland, Oregon, for his investigation exposing a former governor's long concealed sexual misconduct with a 14-year-old girl.

2007 Awarded to **Brett Blackledge** of *The Birmingham (AL) News* for his exposure of cronyism and corruption in the state's two-year college system, resulting in the dismissal of the chancellor. . . .

2009 Awarded to **David Barstow** of *The New York Times* for his tenacious reporting that revealed how some retired generals, working as radio and television analysts, had been co-opted by the Pentagon to make its case for the war in Iraq, and how many of them also had undisclosed ties to companies that benefited from policies they defended.

All the signs of sin are out there, but also the signs of grace. Journalists tell grace stories all the time. Some have become almost routine. People donate their organs to each other and set up organ-giving plans, with incentives, so that somebody will undergo the pain of donating a kidney — perhaps to a stranger. A river floods somewhere in the Midwest and guys from all over the country climb in their pickups and drive for hours to the site so they can do backbreaking volunteer work to help people they do not know. This makes no sense unless God is in the picture. A man with an assault rifle enters the Sandy Hook Elementary School in Newtown, Connecticut, and murders twenty children and six adults. People from all over the country send flowers, teddy bears, Christmas wreaths, candles, sorrowing notes. Many make the trek to Newtown simply, as they say, to "show respect for the victims" by their presence. One dog handler from Chicago brings a team of golden retrievers who are trained as "comfort dogs." Children who have lost schoolmates pet the dogs and speak to them of their losses.[7]

7. http://www.chicagotribune.com/news/local/breaking/chi-local-comfort-dogs-taken-to-connecticut-after-school-massacre-20121216,0,7533873.story.

A woman opens a school in a Godforsaken village in Cameroon, and patiently teaches children to read. A man retires from being a plumber, except that he doesn't retire from plumbing. He volunteers with his church to plumb houses in rural Mississippi for people who had assumed that being poor simply entailed that you had permanently busted plumbing.

The preacher who wants wisdom about sin and grace has unlimited places to go. Journalists live in a lot of these places, but storytellers, too, such as Flannery O'Connor. O'Connor's fiction includes a lot of pain, and you have to absorb some of it in order to read her. Poor people, ignorant people, freakish and loutish and suicidal people — they are all there, and so are the hogs rooting and grunting fifty feet from where people live.

God gets into O'Connor stories sideways. Grace comes in on a slant. It's never boxed or controlled. It's always unpredictable, and it keeps finding the unlikeliest subjects: a boy who figures that if he can get some of Jesus in baptism by immersion, then he can get all of Jesus by drowning.[8] A man named Parker who has survived a tractor crash then wants a symbol of the grace that saved him. So he gets Jesus tattooed onto his back — "the haloed head," says O'Connor, "of a flat stern Byzantine Christ with all-demanding eyes."[9] Parker's wife is a born-again Protestant who finds the tattooed icon idolatrous, and so she beats Parker on his back with her broomstick till welts appear on the face of the suffering Lord.

Sin and grace are in O'Connor and in John Steinbeck, too. In his novel titled *East of Eden* Steinbeck gives us the sociopath Cathy Ames, one of the most accomplished liars in modern fiction.

8. Flannery O'Connor, "The River," in *The Complete Stories of Flannery O'Connor* (New York: Farrar, Straus, and Giroux, 1971), pp. 157-74.
9. Flannery O'Conor, "Parker's Back," in *The Complete Stories of Flannery O'Connor*, p. 522.

Cathy's lies were never innocent. Their purpose was to escape punishment, or work, or responsibility, and they were used for profit. Most liars are tripped up either because they forget what they have told or because the lie is suddenly faced with an incontrovertible truth. But Cathy did not forget her lies, and she developed the most effective method of lying. She stayed close enough to the truth so that one could never be sure. She knew two other methods also — either to interlard her lies with truth or to tell a truth as though it were a lie. If one is accused of a lie and it turns out to be the truth, there is a backlog that will last a long time and protect a number of untruths.[10]

This is genius: "If one is accused of a lie and it turns out to be the truth, there is a backlog that will last a long time and protect a number of untruths." Steinbeck saw deeply into lying and cheating and his wisdom is available to any preacher who wants to become the kind of person on whom nothing is lost. Suppose the preacher has in front of her a text from Scripture about the corruption of the human heart, or the cunning lies of the wicked, or about bearing false witness. Cathy Ames comes to mind and the preacher then goes at her text with conviction, and this is so whether or not she quotes Steinbeck.

Or suppose the text du jour has to do with the grace of God. Now the preacher looks into her storehouse of passages on grace from her reading and comes upon this from Dostoevsky: in *Crime and Punishment* Marmeladov drinks up the family's food and rent money. His teenage daughter Sonya becomes a prostitute to support her mother and siblings. She supports Marmelodov too,

10. John Steinbeck, *East of Eden* (New York: Viking, 1952), p. 85.

which chastens him beyond endurance. In a drunken outburst, Marmeladov says it all to one of his friends:

> This very quart was bought with her money. . . . Thirty kopecks she gave me with her own hands, her last, all she had. . . . She said nothing, only looked at me without a word. . . . Not on earth, but up yonder . . . they grieve over men, they weep, but they don't blame them, they don't blame them! But it hurts more, it hurts more when they don't blame![11]

The grace of God is terrible in its judgment because who can need it but the guilty, but it is also devastating in its mercy, healing the same wound it inflicts. The preacher who wants to say that grace can be more devastating than revenge, and that the pain of God's grace will bring life if we can get through the pain — this preacher will summon to mind Javert or Marmelodov because her message is counter-intuitive, and she will need all the help she can get to bring it home.

"After Them Shitheels"

I have had several occasions earlier in the book to cite John Steinbeck's masterpiece *The Grapes of Wrath*. In it the Joad family leaves their Oklahoma house desolate and heads for California because they have been told there is plenty of work there, and grapes in huge clusters, and little white houses surrounded by little white picket fences. Ma Joad has her heart set on a little white house for *her* family, and you come to understand as you read

---

11. Fyodor Dostoevsky, *Crime and Punishment*, trans. Constance Garnett (New York: Random House, 1956), p. 19.

that a big ingredient in tragedy — the sorrow in it, the poignancy in it — is generated at the point that tender hope gets crushed by brutal reality.

The novel includes a number of so-called inter-chapters, in which Steinbeck pulls the camera back from the Joads on the road to California, and gives us a historical summary of migration in the 1930s, or an overview of the social pressures on migrants and farmers when there are simply too many people who want too few jobs. Sometimes an inter-chapter will give us a little drama that reveals the social conditions migrants faced when trying to sell their possessions or buy a car or stop along the way for food and drink.

In a famous inter-chapter, Steinbeck describes a migrant family who stops at a diner.[12] Al stands hulking over the griddle there and Mae works the counter and two truckers on their stools sit for pie and coffee. A hatchet-faced migrant dad and two barefoot boys walk in. What happens next you never see coming.

The dad approaches Mae. "Could you see your way to sell us a loaf of bread, ma'am?" Mae balks. "This ain't a grocery store. We got bread to make san'widges."

"I know, ma'am," says the man. But we're hungry and "there ain't nothing for quite a piece they say." Mae is still balking. "If I sell you bread we're going to run out. Why'nt you buy a san'widge. We got nice san'widges, hamburgs."

We can't afford san'widges, says the man. We got to make a dime do all of us. Mae resists. "You can't get no loaf a bread for a dime," she says. "We only got fifteen-cent loafs."

And from behind her Al growls, "God Almighty, Mae, give 'em bread." She protests: "We'll run out 'fore the bread truck comes."

---

12. Steinbeck, *The Grapes of Wrath* (New York: Penguin, 2002), pp. 153-62. The part of the chapter I will quote and paraphrase is on pp. 159-62.

"Run out then, goddamn it," says Al, and looks down sullenly at the potato salad he's mixing.

Mae opens a drawer, pulls out a loaf of bread, and says, "This here is a fifteen-cent loaf." The man "answered with inflexible humility. 'Won't you — can't you see your way to cut off ten cents' worth?'"

"Al said snarlingly, 'Goddamn it, Mae, give 'em the loaf.'"

The man reaches into his pouch for a dime and a penny comes out with it. He then notices his two boys in front of the candy case. Steinbeck, in his genius, writes that the boys were staring into the candy case "not with craving or with hope or even with desire, but just with a kind of wonder that such things could be."

The dad is about to drop his penny back into the pouch, but he sees his boys. He turns to Mae. "How much is them sticks of peppermint candy?" he asks. "Is them penny candy, ma'am?"

"The boys had stopped breathing as Mae answers." "No," she says. "Them's not penny candy. Them's two for a penny."

The dad says OK, and he and the boys walk out of the diner to their 1926 Nash, the boys holding their sticks of candy down rigidly at their sides, not able even to look at them.

In the diner, Bill, one of the truckers, wheels around toward Mae. "'Them wasn't two-for-a-cent candy,'" he says. "What's that to you?" says Mae. The truckers each place a coin on the counter and turn to leave. Mae calls at them, "'Hey! Wait a minute. You got change comin.'"

"'You go to hell,'" says Bill, and slams the screen door.

Mae goes to where the truckers had been sitting. She had expected their usual tip — a dime on top of fifteen cents for the pie and coffee. But each man has left her a half dollar.

"Truck drivers," says Mae reverently, as she fingers the coins. "Truck drivers," and right "after them shitheels" took all my bread.

As the scene closes, Al busies himself with rigging slot machine number three so it won't pay off to the next customer who comes through the door.

Our preacher who reads the diner scene in *The Grapes of Wrath* will find wisdom in it. Read the scene and it dawns on you that compassion may lurk just underneath the surface. If a tough guy like Al shows it first, compassion becomes contagious as others take permission. Al, then Mae, then the dad, then the truckers — all find their compassion going off like firecrackers in a string. All because a snarling Al lit the fuse when he said, "Goddamn it, Mae, give 'em the loaf." Compassion with a curse — "Goddamn it," "You go to hell," "them shitheels." Compassion with a curse because maybe compassion is a soft virtue, and people who let themselves show it, even for a moment, then want to take revenge on their softness and brace everything up with a reassuring curse.

Is Grace Sufficient?

Grace is God's generous address to human sin and shame. We have just seen that God inspires human forms of grace, including compassion, and that these may become wonderfully contagious. But sin sometimes seems so bad and so damaging that you begin to wonder whether grace is any match for it. Paul says that the Lord had told him "my grace is sufficient" (2 Cor. 12:9) and I grant you it sounds like a modest claim. My grace is sufficient. No more than that. Just sufficient. But no less than that, either, which means God's grace will outstrip ours.

Every so often you read of a murderer at his sentencing turning to the grieving loved ones of his victim and saying words to this effect: "I'm sorry for the trouble I caused you. Not a day goes by that I don't wish I could undo what I did. I shouldn't have killed her."

"I shouldn't have killed her." Is that little bit of grace anywhere nearly sufficient?

A professor at the University of Michigan, Gordon Beauchamp, wrote a stellar piece in *The American Scholar* in which he muses over all the public apologies that we have witnessed in the last two decades.[13] Japan has apologized to China and Korea for terrors before and during World War II. England has apologized to Ireland for insensitivity to their potato famine in the 1840s. The United States has apologized to the Japanese-Americans it interned during the Second World War and has paid reparations to them or to their descendants. The Catholic Church has issued a great many apologies in the last two decades for everything from its treatment of Galileo to its silence on the condition of the Jews and Gypsies in World War II to clerical sexual abuse of children today.

Apologies everywhere and all of them seemingly too little and too late. Human attempts to address wrongdoing are often so partial, so tiny up against the size of the damage. They seem nowhere nearly sufficient, and we can easily imagine victims of sexual abuse or the grieving loved ones of murder victims saying: "An apology? He thinks *an apology* is going to help?"

An apology never helps. Except when it does. One of America's most prominent advocates for the victims of child sexual abuse, attorney Kelly Clark of Portland, Oregon, reports a time he met the executive head of an athletic club in which a 4-year-old had been molested.[14] The parents of the child were there too and

13. Gordon Beauchamp, "Apologies All Around," *The American Scholar,* Autumn 2007.

14. Kelly Clark, "On Apology and Forgiveness — Part II: An Apology Offered with Grace and Power," www.kellyclarkattorney.com/on-apology-and-forgiveness %E2%80%94part-ii-an-apology-offered-with-grace-and-power/.

didn't know what to expect from the executive. The first move by the executive was to apologize from her heart. She was so honest with the parents, so humble, so visibly upset and contrite that the parents were deeply moved and grateful. The executive's tears of sorrow over her company's failure to protect a little girl did not undo the damage. But it did soften and gratify the hearts of the parents.

Many of us have read some of the documents that came out of the Truth and Reconciliation Commission (TRC) in South Africa. What has impressed me and so many others is one theme in the testimony of victims of apartheid. They say that simply *being heard* was enormously important to them. The TRC did not require the perpetrators to apologize. But it did require from perpetrators applying for amnesty that they tell in detail what they did to victims.

So the perpetrators, even with all their predictable evasions, said what they had done to the victims. The victims then said to the world what they had experienced. The truth was out there for all to hear, and the comfort for victims lay simply in having given a public witness to outrage. This meant more to many of the victims than they could say.

In his diary one of the TRC commissioners, Piet Meiring, tells of a policeman, Eric Taylor, who decided he wanted to go further than simply to acknowledge what he had done. He wanted to apologize to the families of four men he had killed. Some church folk arranged the meeting. The situation called for heartfelt, abject, deeply contrite confession on Taylor's part. What Mr. Taylor actually said in the meeting was this: "I am sorry for a lot that happened." Then he asked the families if they would forgive him.[15]

15. Piet Meiring, *A Chronicle of the Truth Commission* (Vanderbijlpark: Carpe Diem, 1999), pp. 123-27.

The situation called for a full, abject, deeply contrite confession of sin. What the families got was a statement so vague that it's a wonder Taylor even bothered with it. Amazingly, the families seized on Eric Taylor's half-assed confession and found in it the grace of God.

"Thanks be to God that He has answered my prayers," said one woman. "It is a relief."

One of the male relatives shook hands with Eric Taylor. "Thank you," he said. "I told God if He put you in front of me I would shake your hand. I appreciate what you have done here today. I am relieved but not yet fully."

"I am relieved, but not yet fully." Already, but not yet. I find in this statement that even in great sorrow God's grace may be sufficient, and I find in this statement that in great sorrow God's grace will never be *wholly* sufficient till Jesus comes again.

That is because no merely human being can apologize and atone for the sins of the world. And it is because, in too many parts of the world, the bullies are still screaming in their treble voices.

Selected Reading List

Adichie, Chimamanda Ngozi. *Purple Hibiscus.* Chapel Hill: Algonquin Books, 2003.

Berry, Wendell. *Jayber Crow.* Washington, DC: Counterpoint, 2001.

Breslin, Jimmy. *The Short, Sweet Dream of Eduardo Gutierrez.* New York: Crown, 2002.

Caro, Robert. *Master of the Senate,* vol. 3 of *The Years of Lyndon Johnson.* New York: Knopf, 2002.

Endo, Shusaku. *Silence,* trans. William Johnston. New York: Taplinger, 1979.

Friedman, Thomas. *The World Is Flat: A Brief History of the Twenty-first Century.* New York: Picador, 2007.

Frost, Robert. *The Poetry of Robert Frost: The Collected Poems,* ed. Edward Connery Lathem. New York: Henry Holt, 1979. See especially "Home Burial," "The Road Not Taken," "After Apple-Picking," "Two Tramps in Mud Time."

Gorney, Cynthia. "Gambling with Abortion (Why Both Sides Think They Have Everything to Lose)." *Harper's,* November 2004.

Griffin, Peter. "Pool Sharks." *The Atlantic Monthly,* August 1994.

Hansen, Ron. *Mariette in Ecstasy.* New York: HarperCollins, 1991.

This list of sources was chosen for "Imaginative Reading for Creative Preaching" Seminars, 2003–present, hosted by Cornelius Plantinga, Hulitt Gloer, and Scott Hoezee at Calvin College (Summer Seminars); Calvin Theological Seminary; Lutheran Camp Chrysalis, Kerrville, Texas; Snow Mountain Ranch, Granby, Colorado; San Francisco Theological Seminary, San Anselmo, California.

Hoezee, Scott. *Proclaim the Wonder: Engaging Science on Sunday.* Grand Rapids: Baker, 2003.

Hosseini, Khaled. *The Kite Runner.* New York: Riverhead, 2003.

Hurston, Zora Neale. *Their Eyes Were Watching God.* New York: HarperPerennial, 2006.

Jones, Edward P. *The Known World.* New York: Amistad, 2006.

Kafka, Franz. *The Trial,* trans. Edwin and Willa Muir. New York: Vintage, 2001.

Keizer, Garrett. *A Dresser of Sycamore Trees: The Finding of a Ministry.* Boston: D. R. Godine, 2001.

Keizer, Garrett. *The Enigma of Anger.* San Francisco: Jossey-Bass, 2004.

Kenyon, Jane. *Otherwise: New and Selected Poems.* Saint Paul: Graywolf, 1996. See especially "In the Nursing Home," "November Calf," "Let Evening Come," "Having It Out with Melancholy," "Otherwise."

LaMott, Anne. *Traveling Mercies: Some Thoughts on Faith.* New York: Pantheon, 1999.

LaMott, Anne. *Plan B: Further Thoughts on Faith.* New York: Riverhead, 2006.

Long, Thomas G. "Why Jessica Mitford Was Wrong." *Theology Today,* January 1999.

Lowry, Lois. *The Giver.* Boston: Houghton Mifflin, 1993.

Lynch, Thomas. *The Undertaking: Life Studies from the Dismal Trade.* New York: Norton, 2009.

Maclean, Norman. *A River Runs Through It and Other Stories,* with a Foreword by Annie Proulx. Chicago: University of Chicago Press, 2001.

Maxwell, William. *All the Days and Nights: The Collected Stories of William Maxwell.* New York: Vintage, 1995. See especially "What Every Boy Should Know," "The Value of Money," "The Lily-White Boys," "The Front and Back Parts of the House," and most of the tiny "Improvisations," especially "The Carpenter," "The Man Who Had No Friends and Didn't Want Any," "The Woman Who Never Drew Breath Except to Complain," "All the Days and Nights."

McBride, James. *The Color of Water: A Black Man's Tribute to His White Mother.* New York: Riverhead, 2006.

Morrison, Toni. *Beloved.* New York: Knopf, 2006.

Nazario, Sonia. *Enrique's Journey.* New York: Random House, 2007.

Némirovsky, Irène. *Suite Française*, trans. Sandra Smith. New York: Knopf, 2006.

Norris, Kathleen. *Dakota: A Spiritual Geography.* Boston: Houghton Mifflin, 2001.

Norris, Kathleen. *The Quotidian Mysteries: Laundry, Liturgy, and "Women's Work."* New York: Paulist, 1998.

Oates, Joyce Carol, and Robert Atwan, eds. *The Best American Essays of the Century.* Boston: Houghton Mifflin, 2000. See especially H. L. Mencken, "The Hills of Zion"; E. B. White, "Once More to the Lake"; Maya Angelou, "I Know Why the Caged Bird Sings"; Maxine Hong Kingston, "No Name Woman."

O'Connor, Flannery. *The Complete Stories.* New York: Farrar, Straus, and Giroux, 1971. See especially "A Good Man Is Hard to Find," "A Temple of the Holy Ghost," "Good Country People," "Everything That Rises Must Converge," "The Lame Shall Enter First," "Revelation," "Parker's Back."

Orwell, George. *Essays.* Everyman's Library edition. New York: Knopf, 2002. See especially "Shooting an Elephant," "Review of *Mein Kampf* by Adolf Hitler," "My Country Right or Left," "The Freedom of the Press," "Politics and the English Language."

Paterson, Katherine. *The Great Gilly Hopkins.* New York: HarperTrophy, 1987.

Robinson, Marilynne. *Gilead.* New York: Farrar, Straus, and Giroux, 2004.

Salzman, Mark. *Lying Awake.* New York: Vintage, 2000.

Schmidt, Gary. *Lizzie Bright and the Buckminster Boy.* New York: Clarion, 2004.

Schmidt, Gary. *Okay for Now.* New York: Clarion, 2011.

Schmidt, Gary. *The Wednesday Wars.* New York: Clarion, 2007.

Schulevitz, Judith. "Bring Back the Sabbath." *The New York Times* Magazine, March 2, 2003.

Shattuck, Roger. *Forbidden Knowledge: From Prometheus to Pornography.* San Diego: Harcourt Brace, 1997.

Sijie, Dai. *Balzac and the Little Chinese Seamstress,* trans. Ina Rilke. New York: Anchor, 2002.

Steinbeck, John. *The Grapes of Wrath.* New York: Penguin, 2002.

Trillin, Calvin. *Remembering Denny.* New York: Warner, 1993.

Updike, John, and Katrina Kenison, eds. *The Best American Short Stories of the Century.* Boston: Houghton Mifflin, 1999. See especially John Cheever, "The Country Husband"; Joyce Carol Oates, "Where Are You Going, Where Have You Been?"; Raymond Carver, "Where I'm Calling From"; Tim O'Brien, "The Things They Carried."

Von Drehle, David. *Triangle: The Fire That Changed America.* New York: Atlantic Monthly, 2003.

Winner, Lauren. *Girl Meets God: On the Path to a Spiritual Life.* Chapel Hill: Algonquin, 2002.

Note to Readers Who Are Preachers or Love Preachers

My co-hosts and I selected the works above, but we did it with lots of help from seminar members, who often recommended something we would schedule in a later seminar. Of course we also got help in the usual places—book reviews in major papers and magazines, word-of-mouth from well-read friends, and various online sources, including http://www.aldaily.com/. We've come to believe that it's wise to get to know local children's librarians and teachers of literature in middle and high schools. They know what fascinates young readers. This knowledge is golden to preachers who hope to reach them—and their parents and grandparents—on Sunday mornings.

What's as important as good things to read is taking the time to harvest, store, and retrieve striking things from the sources in an easily searchable database (I use Pro-Cite). Sometimes it's a pain to do it—and particularly when you're tired—but even five items stored per week will soon enough build into an impressive and supportive treasury, ready and waiting for the day you need it. And, some of the time, you will enjoy harvesting and storing because what you are storing that day is so blamed *good.*

Virtually everything in this book that's any good came from my database.

What you want to store there is anything striking, anything

that has a particularity, an angularity, a twist. This might be the diner scene from *The Grapes of Wrath*, but it might also be something you notice at a local basketball game, or a snippet of wisdom snagged from conversation with a shrewd observer of the human scene ("Have you ever noticed that when people want to . . . ?"). It might be an ad for a wedding dress or a short plot summary from an episode of *Mad Men*.

As I write these lines I'm looking at an article in *Time* magazine[1] about the mysteries of hospital billing, and how a straight question ("Why does a one-inch square alcohol swab, of which you can get a box of a hundred for $3.99 at Wal-Mart, need to cost $6.00 each in the hospital?") will almost never get a straight answer from a hospital administrator. Why is this? Entering the article's main revelations into my database, I will want to tag them with retrievers ("frustration," "medical costs," "systemic evil," and certainly "evasion"). Is there an innocent explanation for what looks to patients like irrationally bloated hospital bills? I hope so. But the evasions are not encouraging along this line. Usually, innocent explanations come forward right away to dispel suspicion.

The comfort in having a database full of juicy stuff is that when the day comes to preach on, say, compassion ("Clothe yourselves with compassion . . .") you already have insights, stories, observations, so that not only you but also your sermon can get clothed with compassion. The idea here is this: you do an honest job of exegesis, and you run your exegeted text through your hermeneutical filters, and you sketch a sermon design. Now, bearing in mind that the Esteé Lauder perfume company suggests that wearers spray a mist into the air and then "walk through it," what you want to do is to spray your juicy stuff on compassion into the

1. Steven Brill, "Bitter Pill," *Time*, March 4, 2013.

air and then walk your exegeted text through it. Maybe something fragrant will cling.

But, apart from sermon illustrations, your reading has made you wiser about compassion. Before reading the diner scene in *The Grapes of Wrath* it hadn't really occurred to me that compassion often lies just below the surface; and that if a tough guy shows it first, the compassion becomes contagious as others take permission; and that, noticing how "soft" they're being, compassionate persons might slap themselves back to "reality" with a few reassuring curses. Steinbeck understood this very human phenomenon and wrote it into his scene. I learned it from him. And I'm glad I did.

One last question for preachers: Do you think you simply don't have enough time to read? But what if a program of general reading would measurably strengthen your preaching? What if, like Eugene Peterson, you begin to schedule reading periods as sermon prep time? What if some of the things that otherwise take your time can be delegated while sermon prep time cannot? Sunday sermons remain, for most of us, the single biggest ministry of the week to the most congregants. Wouldn't that make sermon preparation a top priority? Along with whatever strengthens it?